I0752993

SWEET SIMPLICITY

SWEET SIMPLICITY

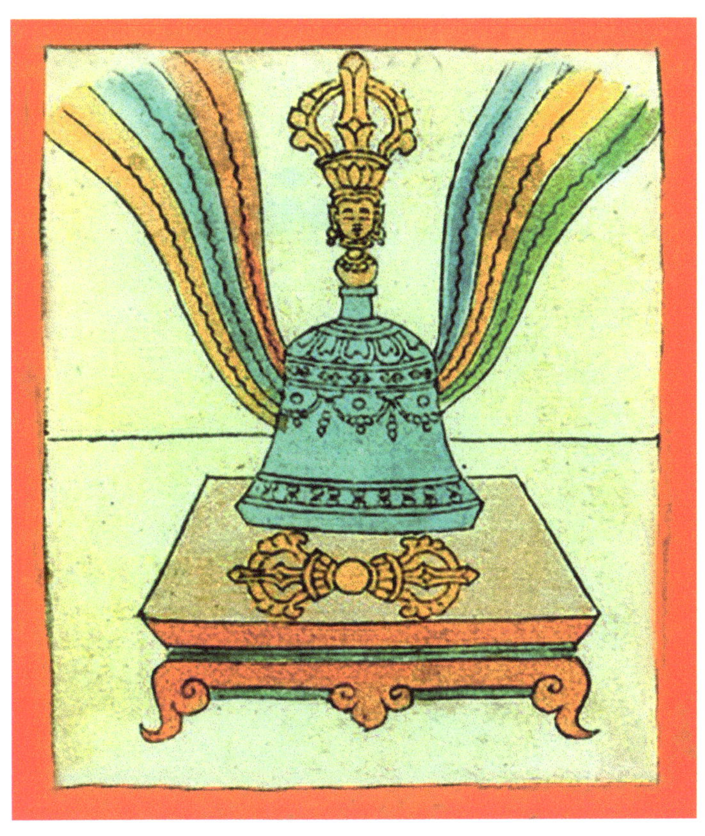

Published by Simply Being www.simplybeing.co.uk

British Library Cataloguing in Publication Data. A catalogue record for this book is available from the British Library.

ISBN: 978-1-7399381-5-4

Cover image and other images are taken from the *Himalayan Art Resources* (*https://www.himalayanart.org/*) which kindly makes their resources available for personal, educational and non-commercial use. Maitripa image: http://tibetanbuddhistencyclopedia.com/en/images/d/d8/Maitripa254.JPG. Flower painting by Diana Collins.

Layout by Sarah Allen.

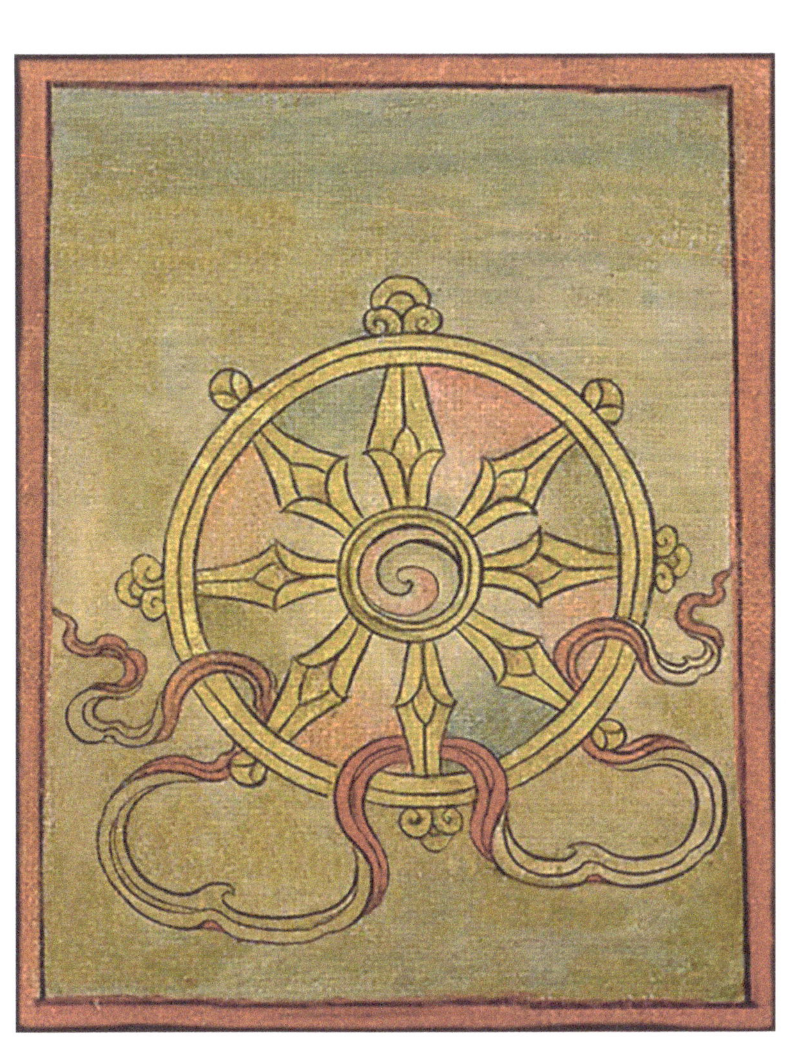

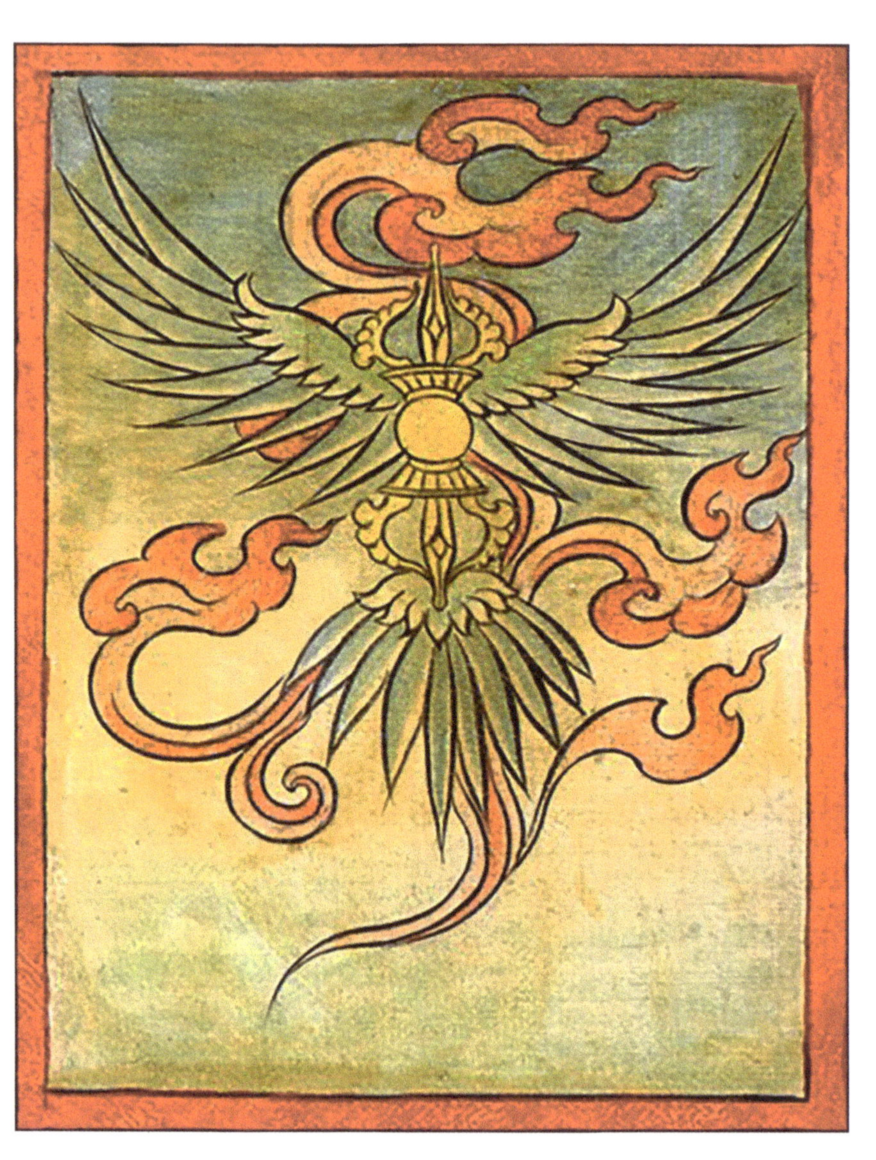

CONTENTS

HOMAGE TO THE GURU
GIFT OF MAHAMUDRA

PURE UNBORN
GENTLE DAWN
DANCING STORM
WE BOW TO YOU

PREFACE

This is a book about being at ease as you are. It has little advice about improving yourself or striving for a distant goal. Yet it is not an encouragement for complacency or self-satisfaction. To be at ease as you actual are is quite different from being at ease with yourself. Our familiar sense of self is unreliable for it is a deluding fabrication, the fruit of our many many efforts to exist. We do not exist. We are not a thing. We are not real. We are the presence of the primordial Buddha. When we stop inventing our transient identities we find a gap, a space in which we can see the unborn openness of our ground, inseparable from its illuminating clarity within which we move in our apparitional patternings. The integrity of these three aspects is called Mahamudra. Since it is always already how it is there is no lack and so no need to add anything, and no excess and so no need to remove anything.

As Tilopa said in his *Six Words of Advice to Naropa*,

No recollection:	don't call back what has gone
No imagining:	don't call forth what may come
No considering:	don't think about what is occurring now
No analysing:	don't look for hidden meaning
No meditating:	don't cultivate anything
No straying:	simply at ease here and now

The first eight texts in this book come from a very well known collection, the Eight Treasuries of Dohas. These doha songs are treasuries, stores of precious clarity. The words are the container, the key is our attention and receptivity. When the key turns the lock of opacity is undone and the true treasure, liberating clarity, flows into our lives.

I began translating these text with C. R. Lama in 1976 but other tasks left this work incomplete. The lock down of 2020 gave me a chance to translate everything in this book. Many thanks are due to Barbara Terris for typing the translations. Sarah Allen formatted them for this book and did the design with enthusiasm and flair.

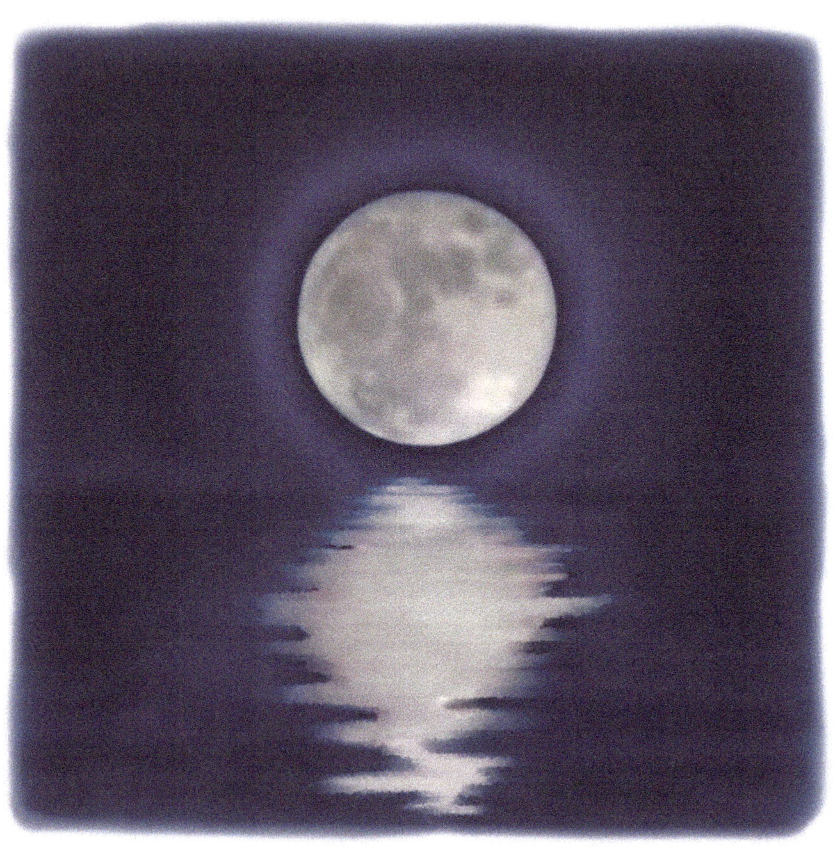

INTRODUCTION

When we look around us we see much that is beautiful and much that is ugly. When we observe ourselves we may well see the same. Some people seem to see only beauty and others seem to see only ugliness – both within themselves and outside. What we see as beautiful someone else may well see as ugly. Reflecting on this we might get a sense that we are part of what we see, that our experience is filtered through the layers of our habits, expectations, degrees of attention and distraction, levels of emotional arousal, amount of sleep and many other factors. These factors are unstable in their impact as they are both fluctuating in their presence and mutually influencing.

Our experience is not what we think it is. It is not a straightforward account of how life is. Our subjectivity projects interpretations onto and into all that we encounter. Subject and object are born together, mutually conditioning and endlessly elaborating. Even if we seem to be satisfied with our situation and complacent in our assumptions of reassuring continuity, the flow of the contents of our mind, both conscious and unconscious, are endlessly at work forming fresh patterns for us to believe in.

It is a strange fact that the seeming order and givenness of our experience rests on random disorder. When we sit with our mind and do not feed it distraction with movements of our body and speech, we find a chaotic display of events that often have little in common. A memory, a plan, a sensation, arising and passing – some hooking our involvement, others arousing indifference or aversion. When we allow ourselves to truly see this we may well be shocked. 'If this is how I am then who am I?' The seemingly fairly stable continuity of our sense of self is based on the mask of identity, the patterning of our ego-self. This dynamic formation of the felt sense of our 'existence' is ceaselessly cultivated, planted and weeded. This seeming continuity of self-identity is revealed through our personality, our postures, gestures, tone of voice, vocabulary, and in the items and areas of attention and value we find in the environments we move through.

Our ego's need for self-maintenance requires two factors: a belief in the existence of separate entities that can be made use of, and more fundamentally a belief in the real existence of ourselves as an entity, as an enduring someone with the unique specificity of I, me, myself. Both of these beliefs are deceptive for they rest on the unobserved process of reification, of constructing graspable 'things' out of the ungraspable flow of occurrence. Believing in existents, in things having their own inherent existence, we are unaware of the basic field within which we are. This field or sphere of openness is our true source and it has never been contaminated by our delusion that we have our own real existence, our own personal defining identity.

The texts in this short book all point out that liberation from the suffering of samsara lies in awakening to this unchanging ground. Since this ground openness is not a thing and all our languages rest on the imagined existence of things, it is beyond description. Yet in their kindness the Buddhas, yogis and siddhas have offered their expressions of how the authentic manifests for them. Although diverse dharma vocabularies have developed over the generations of the transmission it is vital not to reify the key terms and imagine that dharmata, dharmadhatu, dharmakaya and so on refer to real places or substances. Words are like waves on the inexpressible ocean. The waves have diverse shapes yet the essence they manifest is the same and is intrinsically inexpressible. If we see the non-difference or non-duality of 'as is' and 'as if' then we can learn to playfully swim in the ocean of dharma without being buffeted by the waves or wasting our time trying to control them.

This book is about Mahamudra. Mahamudra is one of many words indicating your mind as it is. As it is it is the non-duality of ungraspable emptiness, the ever-fecund openness free of selectivity, and ungraspable luminosity, the bright potential of all that can appear, inherently free of things and their nouns. Our mind is not a thing. I am not a thing. Thingness is a way of thinking arising from unawareness of the non-duality of emptiness and appearance. When emptiness is disregarded we have the birth of the ego-self, a pretender, an actor, a specialist in make-believe. With this, appearances are mistaken to be the appearance of something. Each something seems to possess its own essence or underpinning inherent existence that sets this 'thing' apart from that 'thing'. I am not you. You are you and I am me. We are two not one – and no amount of romantic fantasy will make us 'one'.

Luminosity is the inherent radiance of the mind. This has two aspects, clear light and the light of colouration. Clear light is the basic potential of revelation, the illumination of the open sky, the bright infinity of emptiness. This is appearance at its simplest – bright light, ungraspable, indefinable, inexpressible. This is 'as is', the unaltering ground and source of all. The light of colouration is formalised in the buddhist traditions as light of five colours, white, red, blue, yellow and green. This formalisation should not be taken as restrictive. All appearance is the light of colouration – not only colours but smells, tastes, sounds, sensations and so on. All the diversity of occurrence is the light of colouration which is inseparable from clear light which is inseparable from emptiness. Each occurrence occurs and vanishes where it occurs. This site is called dharmata, the empty truth of phenomena. They do not leave this. They are unborn, having no separate existence, and are undying since being unborn there is no entity to die. This immediacy of each and all is hidden from us only by the ego's need to grasp and reify. All is received without effort when nothing is taken.

The traditional Indian term for this is sahaj, the directness of non-creation and non-construction. The empty ground and its non-dual display are simultaneous, co-emergent, arising together. Although the empty ground never actually arises, it is as if it does as appearance since it is inseparable from that appearance. This non-duality is known as Mahamudra, the great seal or symbol or gesture. Non-duality seals all appearance within emptiness so that there is not an atom of autonomous existence to be apprehended. Thus it points to the futility of grasping and the absence of any need for effort. Symbols and gestures speak without speaking and this points to the non-conceptual quality of this view, meditation and activity. The division or separation of appearance and emptiness is an illusion, the excitation of there being something there. When we see an illusion like a mirage to be an illusion, we are instantly released from the delusion that there is a real entity there. Samsara is just such an illusion. To see that it is unborn is to heal the wound that has never occurred. With the clarity of this view there is no need for formal meditation. Awareness of the ungraspability of phenomena does not interfere with or cover up their spontaneous self-liberation. No making of entities means no need to get rid of entities. Activity then flows easily from this. Since the ego dissolves in the light of luminosity like night with the rising sun, there is no self-referential distortion to our being in the world with others and we find ourselves as participants in the common good, freely manifesting as required.

Although the key point is that there is nothing to be done in order to 'make liberation happen', because we are so used to having maps to give us a sense of direction some general 'maps' have developed in the lineages of Mahamudra. Although there is nowhere to go and nothing to be done this sweet invitation can seem brutal to those who face a rapid detoxification from their love-affair with duality. Therefore it can be useful to have the overview of the often described four stages or aspects.

The first is one-pointedness. This is the capacity to remain undistracted whatever happens. Clear that there is nothing to gain or lose, no arising has anything to offer in terms of help or harm. Appearance is empty in essence and so living or dying becomes equal. It is our attachments that set these as polar opposites. Whatever comes, comes. Whatever goes, goes. Simply rest in one-pointed presence in the ungraspable present.

The second aspect is simplicity or freedom from elaboration. When an event occurs, whether seemingly mental or environmental, leave it as it is. It is what it is, as it is. If you conceptualise it you are likely to do something with it. We elaborate by installing the concept of the event in one of our many frames of reference, especially the polarities of creation and cessation, nihilism and eternalism, coming and going, differentiation and homogenisation. These polarities allow for the rapid allocation of value and this arouses the five afflicting poisons of opacity, desire, aversion, pride and jealousy. Now we are immersed in an affective relationship with something that concerns us. All of this is the unnecessary activity of the mind when the mind is unaware of its own empty essence. So we simply have to relax and release, let the mind be as it is, empty open awareness, and let the mind's radiance be as it is, empty bright appearance of nothing. This is simplicity.

The third aspect is one-taste. This is a quality of non-complication, of freeing ourself from the need to put our opinion on everything. When the arising mental event is seen for what it is, an empty signifier signifying emptiness, we are no longer enticed into commenting on ourselves, on others, and on the world we encounter. Everything has the same taste, the taste of the non-duality of emptiness and luminosity. We are free from the egoic need for story-telling as we are no longer maintaining our lives with stories. Freed from the imprisoning creativity of Scheherazade, words, stories, and plans become the play of light. Nothing is at stake and so we are released from seriousness. This frees the energy we manifest, the quality of the light of colouration, to respond to what is vital in the actual situation. Free of the burden of identifying differentiating qualities and then attributing value leading to necessary action, we are more open to the rich potential of the world. With this we find ourselves effortlessly resourced and so are able to jettison anxious striving. One-taste is not bland, nor, paradoxically, is it homogenised. Diversity is not other than one taste for diversity has the one taste of emptiness without losing its flavour and savour.

The fourth aspect is non-meditation. We usually think that there is something that we have to do in order to achieve our goal. If we do not do it we will not get the result we seek. However with the support of one-pointedness, simplicity and one-taste, we are starting to relax and trust. Whatever occurs is the occurrence of the ground. That's all. No matter what we or others say or think. It is as it is, inseparable from emptiness. Therefore what is to be removed? What is to be added? Each moment of relaxed presence is complete in itself. Free of lack or excess there is no need for the ego's busy involvement and its self-sustaining activity of adopting and rejecting. Finally the ego is redundant, retired from duty. We are living in the spontaneity of sahaj – fully present to the complexity of occurrence yet simultaneously not straying from its simplicity. We are freed from conceptual complications and our meditation is simply to abide in the presence of ever-open awareness whether we are sitting or moving, eating or sleeping. The energy of luminosity has no need of any artificial doer or maker.

The integrity of these four factors reveals the uncontrived always already complete Mahamudra that is our own mind. Opening to these intrinsic qualities of the mind as it is we gradually release the fear and anxiety arising from identification with the ego-self. This ego-self has no inherent existence: it is an energy whorl sucking in fresh arisings as a means to replenish its ever-vanishing actuality. As we relax and rest in our unborn openness, the habit of clinging declines until the tension of isolation dissolves and we are present in the unchanging integrity of Mahamudra. Tensing is a dualistic activity and has many methods and pathways. Relaxing and releasing is, in its true mode, a non-dualistic non-activity. We each have to get to know our own specific knots and tensions and desist from intensifying them. There is no 'way to do it' because it is a non-doing.

It is therefore vital that when we read the doha songs of awakening in this book we do not use them as a criticism of how we currently find ourself nor as a goad to transform ourselves. These dohas are gentle encouragements to trust the fundamental purity, goodness and wholeness of our mind as it is. Letting go of false and unnecessary agitation we find that the non-duality of subject and object, of self and other, gives rise to spontaneous connectivity imbued with kindness. Having no need of ego gain, there is effortless harmonising collaboration with whatever arises, minimising the mutually excluding difference that leads to conflict. With non-dual awareness the whole heals itself from a wound that has never occurred and the rich variety of occurrence allows the pliable responsivity of luminosity to manifest our presence as required.

There are now many books available in English on Mahamudra and if you wish you can learn about its history and the lives of the great siddha yogis. You can also find erudite commentaries on many of the dohas offered here. I do not wish to add further explanations for perhaps the texts need space and silence free of concepts so that they can breathe their life into us.

The key focus for our attention should be our own mind. Concepts are beguiling and deceptive. They give us tools for thinking about what is happening. This feeds the ego and veils our own intrinsic awareness. We need less knowledge about and more direct opening to. We sit with muscles relaxed as our skeleton takes our weight. Breath is easy, unforced and carried by the gentle pulse of the diaphragm. Our senses are open but not locked on to objects. Appearances come and go. Not interfering in this free flow we release our habits of selection, of adopting and rejecting.

When we read these dohas we are not seeking to extract gold. They are all gold. Some parts will speak to you more than others on particular days. However it is perhaps more beneficial to attend evenly to the whole otherwise we are enacting another aspect of selectivity, like only listening to the great arias and ignoring the rest of the opera. In the land of gold everything is gold. The evenness of the object side and the equanimity of the subject side collaborate to prevent splitting, grasping and pre-occupation. When everything is special there are no special events. One taste in diversity allows each moment to bathe us in sweet simplicity.

Opening ourselves to these doha songs we are welcomed into our presence as awareness of the non-duality of emptiness and luminosity. Absorbing the blessing of the mood of awakening our awareness is freed from constructing meaning on the basis of the words. These songs were often sung at gathering feasts of yogis where the ripeness of the participants meant that no further explanation was necessary. Reading them, and especially reading them out loud, lets the sound vibration soften our knotted pathways so that the pulse of connectivity is unobstructed and we find ourselves in and as non-dual presence. When we walk in nature we do not need to know the names of all the flowers and trees. In fact by not fitting them into our pre-established templates we offer ourselves the joy of seeing with fresh eyes the fresh ungraspable beauty of the world. So as we read and recite these dohas the binary of knowing and not knowing can be released so that our fresh open heart finds its own sweet simplicity.

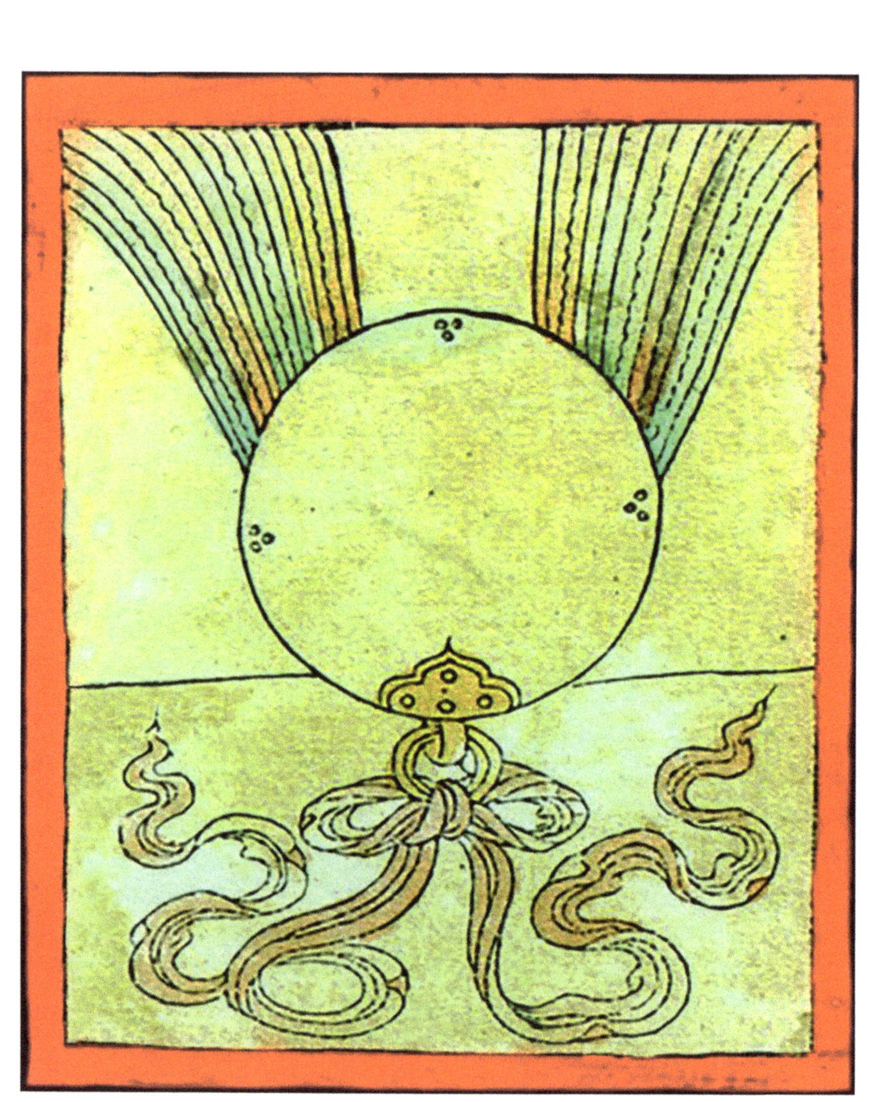

SECTION 1

THE EIGHT TREASURIES OF DOHA SONGS WHICH ELUCIDATE THE ESSENTIAL INSTRUCTIONS ON MAHAMUDRA

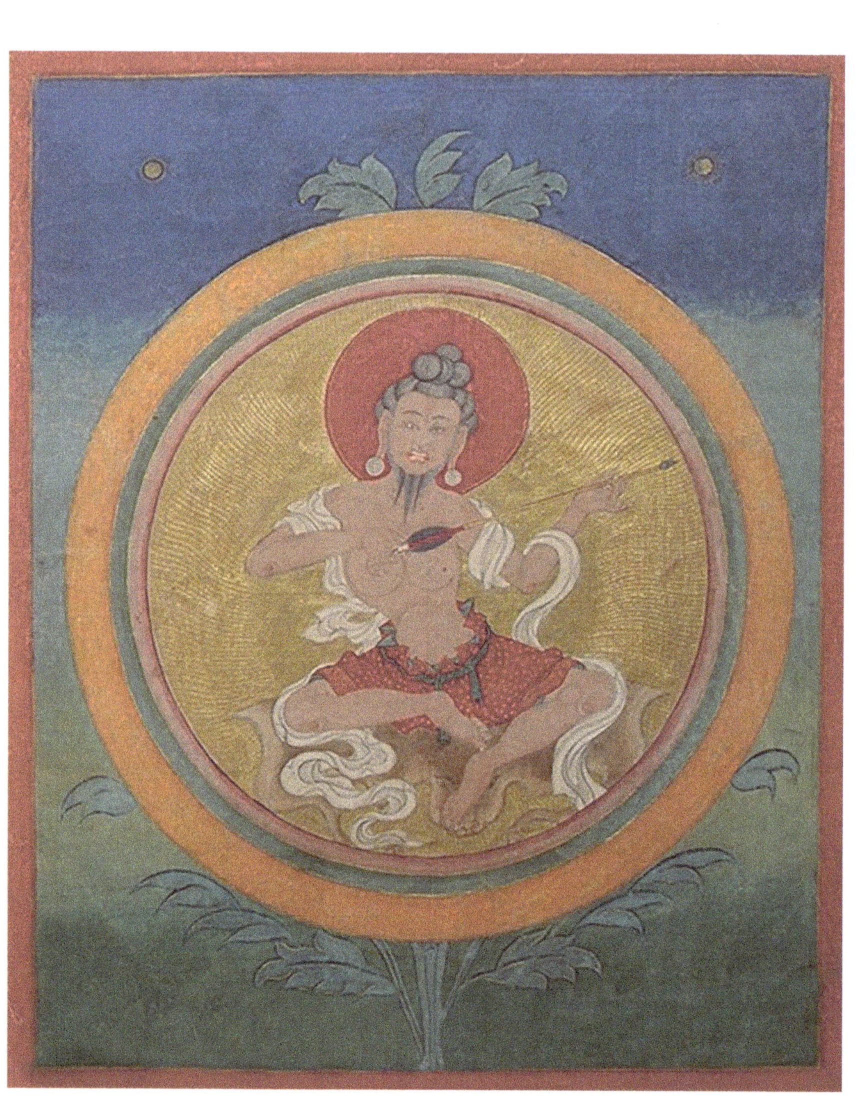

THE DOHA TREASURY OF MAHAMUDRA INSTRUCTIONS OF SARAHA

IN THE LANGUAGE OF INDIA: *DOHA GANAMA MAHAMUDRA UPADESA*

IN THE LANGUAGE OF TIBET: *DO HA MDZOD CES BYA BA PHYAG RGYA CHEN PO'I MAN NGAG*

I pay homage to Sri Vajradakini!
I pay homage to the great bliss innate original knowing!

The topics of this text are presented in three sections.

SECTION 1. SHOWING MAHAMUDRA AS IT IS

This has three aspects: A, B and C.

A. EXPLAINING HOW IT ABIDES

Animate and inanimate, moving and non-moving,
Substantial and insubstantial, appearance and emptiness—
Everything, without exception, during all time
Never deviates from the nature of space.

Although you repeat, 'space', 'space'
The essence of space has no reality at all.
Existing, not existing, neither existing nor not existing,
Or something else— it transcends being any such object.

Thus 'space', 'mind', 'actuality'
Have not the least difference.
All names indicating difference are just incidental labelling.
They are nothing but meaningless false words.

All phenomena are one's own mind.
Other than one's own mind
There is not even an atom of an entity.
Whoever awakens to the primordial non-existence of mind
Gains the holy vision of the victors of the three times.

It is well named as 'the casket of dharma'.
It is not some other mistaken dharma,
Being the primordial innate essence.
The thusness of this is not something that can be taught:
Being beyond expression, no one can understand it.

If there is an owner there will be possessions,
Yet from the beginning there has been no self
So what could it possibly possess?
If the mind exists as something
Then all phenomena will exist as something.
If the mind does not exist who would be able to know phenomena?

All that appears as mind and phenomena
Are not found if sought for and there is no seeker anywhere.
Non-existent they are unborn and unceasing in the three times.
Thusness does not become something else,
It abides as it is, natural great bliss.

Therefore all appearances are the dharmakaya,
All sentient beings are buddhas.
From the beginning all composition and karmic activity
Is the dharmadhatu:
All identified phenomena are like the horns on a hare.

B. Beings are deluded through not awakening to the actual

Alas! The light rays of the unclouded sun are all-pervading
Yet for the blind darkness is the constant appearance.
The innate pervades everything
Yet for the stupefied thusness is far away.

Because beings are not awake to the non-existence of mind
Mind itself is strongly bound by their discriminating minds.
Just as one can become mad by the influence of demons and then
Powerlessly, meaninglessly, create suffering,
Grasped by the great demon of reification and conceptualisation
Beings create only meaningless suffering.

Some of the stupefied are bound up in intellectual classification.
They leave the master at home and seek him elsewhere.
Some take reflections to be real.
Some leave the root and cut the leaves.
Whatever they do, they do not notice they are deceived.

C. How this hermit awakes

Ah! Although the childlike are unaware of thusness,
I am aware that they have never strayed from the state of thusness.
I have seen my beginning and my end.
I have seen I: this I alone remains.

I look at this alone itself and this one is not to be seen.
Without seer or seen, it is inexpressible.
Since it is inexpressible, who can understand it?

When the original mind is fully available
You will enter my, the hermit's, awakening.
A lioness's milk cannot be kept in an ordinary pot.

Just as in the forest the roar of a lion
Makes all the small deer terrified
Yet the lion cubs happily run towards it,

Teaching this great bliss unborn from the very beginning
Makes the stupefied and mistaken terrified
Yet the fortunate are happy and their body hair vibrates.

Section 2. The path of mahamudra

This has three aspects, A, B and C.

A. View: Being certain through the view

This has three aspects:

A1. Showing the view as it is

Ah! With an unwavering mind, by yourself look at yourself.
When you awaken to your own thusness
Even the wavering mind arises as mahamudra.
Conceptual identification self-liberates in the state of great bliss.

Happiness and suffering occurring in dreams
Are unreal while one is awake,
Thus abandoning all hopeful and fearful attitudes
Who is there to entertain thoughts of preventing and accomplishing?

All the phenomena of samsara and nirvana
Have no reality when thusness is seen and so
Attitudes of hope and fear are ended.
So who will strive at rejecting and adopting?

Every appearance and sound is like an illusion, a mirage,
A reflection, and thus lacks the characteristics of real entities.
The one wise to this illusory appearance is the mind itself;
Like space it lacks limit and centre, and so who can know it?

Just as the various rivers such as the Ganges
Will have one taste in the salty ocean,
The discriminating mind and all that occurs for it
Is known to have one taste in the dharmadhatu.

A2. The manner of awakening

Someone may thoroughly search the entire extent of space
Yet, seeing that it is without limit or centre,
Their search ceases completely.
In the same way, if one thoroughly searches for mind and phenomena
Not even an atom of essence can be found.
The mind that thoroughly searches
Also cannot be found as something and thus
One sees that is there is nothing whatsoever to see.

A3. Not straying from this

Just as a crow flying away from a ship
Circles in all directions and returns again to it
The desiring mind may chase after thoughts
Yet returns to the authentic original mind itself.
Not affected by conditions, finished with hopes,
The hiding place of fears is destroyed— this is the vajra mind.

B. Meditation: there are two aspects to this

B1. The non-meditation of mahamudra

Mind itself cuts the root and is like space.
Being free of meditation there is no activity for mentation.
Ordinary mind in its authentic intrinsic mode
Is unadulterated by contrived objectification.
The naturally pure mind has no need of artifice.
Not holding, not releasing, leave the mind as it is.
If the unawakened intellect has no cause for meditation
With awakening there is no object of meditation and no meditator.

In as much as space is not an object for space,
Emptiness likewise does not meditate on emptiness.
Knowing non-duality is like water and milk.
Diversity has one taste, uninterrupted great bliss.

B2. The supreme meditation inseparable from the presence of non-meditation

In this way, throughout all the three times,
There is the limitless authentic state free of mental activity.
'Meditation' is the conventional term used for the protection of this.
Do not hold the breath, do not bind the mind.
Settle uncontrived awareness as you would a baby.
If memories and thoughts arise look at their thusness.
Do not think of water and waves as separate.

B3. Examples illustrating the mahamudra path of unapprendable ordinary mind itself, free of the three wheels

With mahamudra, the non-activation of mentation,
There is not an atom of cause for meditation so do not meditate.
The supreme meditation never separates
From the presence of non-meditation.

Non-dual, innate, the taste of great bliss:
In as much as water poured into water has one taste
When you dwell in that way in such a state
The mentation that desires objectification and grasping is no more.

C. Conduct: there are three aspects to this

C1. Mahamudra conduct is not pre-set

Oh! For yogis of authentic non-duality
What entities are there to be adopted or rejected?
I neither hold to nor discard any phenomena and so
I do not say, "You, my child, must do this!"

Just as that jewel, the mind, is unreal,
So the conduct of the yogi is unreal.
Although his talk is idle chatter and diverse stories,
The yogi's mind does not stray from singularity.

This singularity itself has no existence as one thing, and so
As the diverse appearances are without root,
Like a madman, carefree and unconstrained,
Maintain child-like conduct free of intentional activity!

C2. How to avoid being tainted by circumstances when behaving in this way

Wondrous! The mind is like a lotus growing from the mud of samsara:
There is no fault that can in any way stain it.
Food, drink and sexual contact bring pleasure
Yet body and mind can also be tormented by them.
So no matter what you make use of
Be untainted, neither bound nor freed by anything.

C3. Spontaneous desireless compassion benefiting others

With the carefree state of the uncontrived conduct of awakening
When stupefied beings experience torment
The force of overwhelming compassion brings tears.
Self takes the place of the other and true benefit occurs.

Analysing the true actuality
One is free of reifying subject, object and their connection,
Unreal, they are like dreams and illusion.
Being free of desire and involvement one is happy and free of sorrow
Like a master magician working with the truth of illusion.

Section 3: The immediacy of mahamudra

This has three aspects: A, B and C.

A. The certainty of gaining the result

The nature of space is primordial purity
Without the least entity to be gained or discarded.
Non activation of mentation is mahamudra
So do not discard anything for the sake of the result.

The mind that hopes has been unborn from the very beginning.
So what could there be to be discarded or gained?
If someone were to get something real
What would we do with the teachings of the four mudras?

B. The delusion of desiring something when there is nothing to get

Just as a deluded mountain deer tormented by thirst
Races towards the water it sees in a mirage
So stupefied beings tormented by desire
Find that the harder they try the further away their goal becomes.

C. Gaining absolutely nothing is called 'the attainment of Vajradhara'

Unborn from the very beginning, the completely pure presence
Has not the least difference within it.
Discriminating mentation is pure appearance within space.
This is called 'Vajradhara', a mere name.

Just as with a mirage appearing in a dry desert
Water appears yet there is no actual water at all.
So discriminating mentation is purified on primordial purity and
Cannot be spoken of as the duality of permanence and annihilation.

As with the wish-fulfilling jewel and the wish-granting tree,
Through the power of aspiration hopes are completely fulfilled.
Moreover this world is conventional only, and within relative truth.
There is nothing truly existing in absolute truth.

This completes *The Mahamudra Instructions: The Doha Treasury* which came from the mouth of the glorious hermit Saraha. It was translated by the Indian scholar Vairocana (Rakshita)

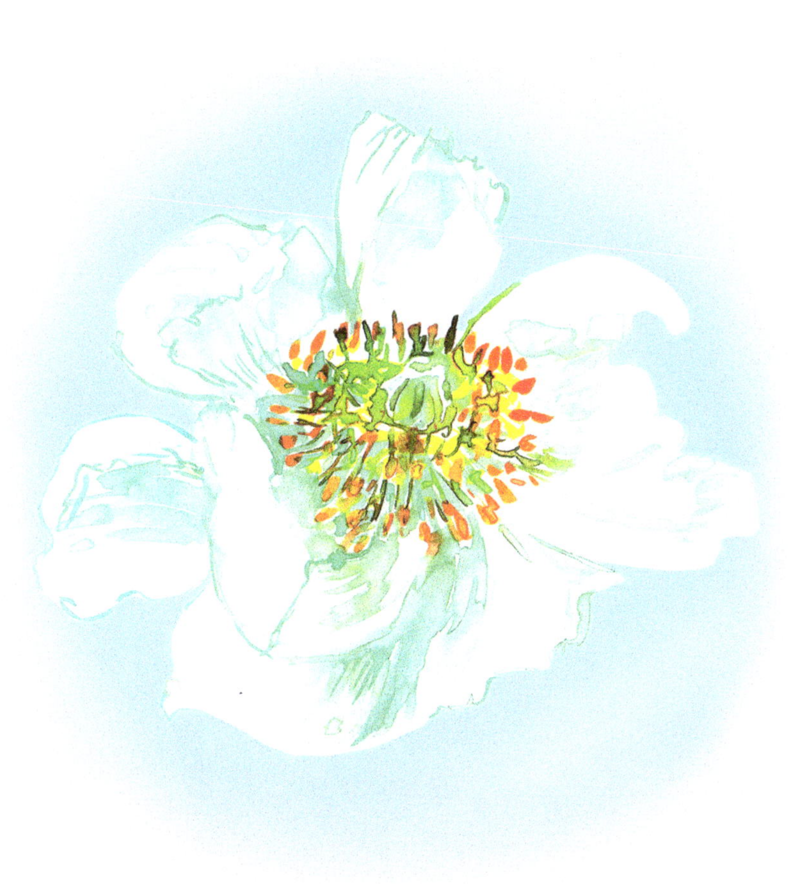

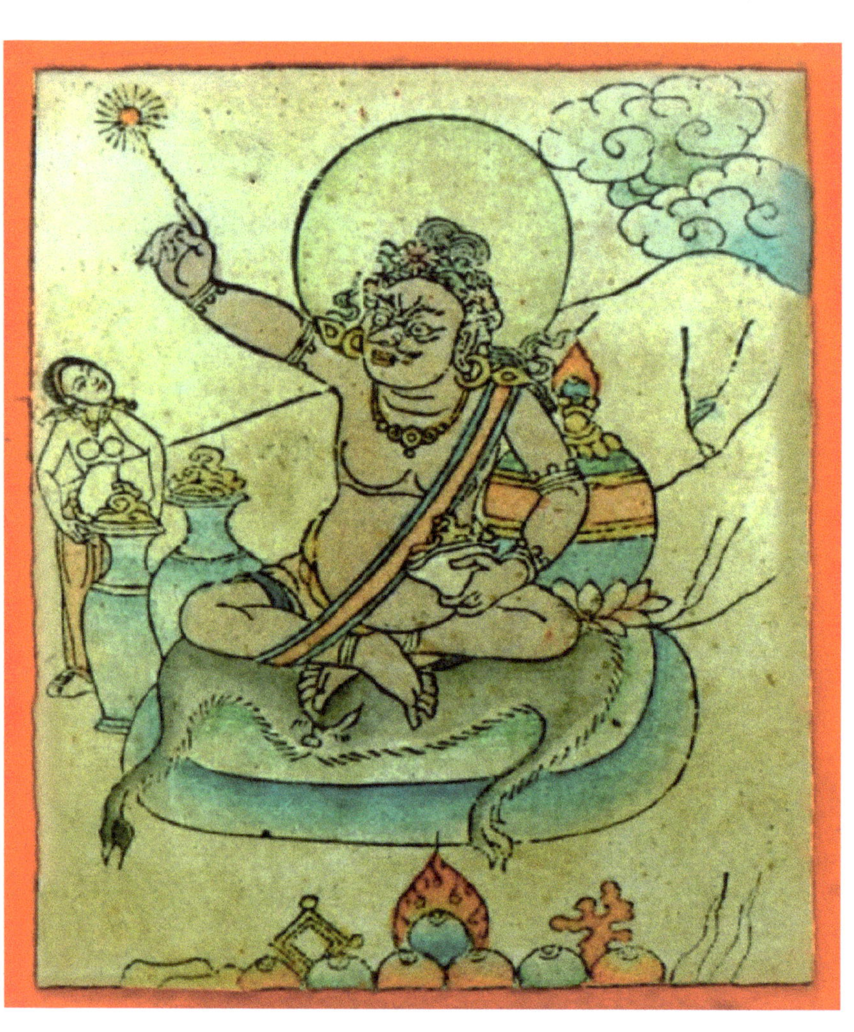

THE DOHA TREASURY OF VIRUPA

IN THE LANGUAGE OF INDIA: DOHAKOSANAMA

IN THE LANGUAGE OF TIBET: DO HA MDZOD CES BYA BA

I pay homage to Sri Vajrasattva!
I pay homage to Bhagavati Nairatmya!

This song has three parts:

A. The absolute truth mahamudra which is how the ground abides

B. The relative truth mahamudra which shows the way

C. The immediacy of the inseparability of these two truths

A. Presenting how the absolute is

Wondrous! Mahamudra, the equality of samsara and nirvana,
Is inherently unborn and completely pure like space.
How it is cannot be indicated and so
The pathway of conventional terms is cut.
Naturally inexpressible
It is essentially free of association with phenomena.

Beyond designation, examination and illustrative examples,
Evading all examples, its non-dwelling
Offers nothing for the intellect.
Neither eternal nor extinguished
It is of neither samsara nor nirvana.
It is neither appearance nor emptiness,
Neither substantial nor insubstantial – and it is not unborn.

It is not the innate truth of phenomena.
It is not a transcendence of the intellect.
Neither 'is not' nor 'is', it cannot be described by the intellect
And hence, not connected with any dualistic phenomena,
It always abides in evenness.
Although its essence, descriptions and functions are explained
This is like explaining the imagined sharpness or bluntness
Of the imagined horns on a hare.
The characteristics of all phenomena do not differ from this.

In this way, all the relative (truth) phenomena
Which are taken to appear and exist
Have no individual essence and are
Merely names, symbols and signs.
Such names and inferred meanings
Establish no true difference between them.
Innately This, from the very beginning
There is nothing to seek elsewhere.

The mind is itself an empty naming;
Beyond conceptualising, it is mahamudra.
Thus it resembles the nature of space
Which has always been just an empty name.
Unborn through its very essence
It is not an entity with characteristics.
All pervasive like space it does not change or move away.
It is always completely empty and is
Primordially without separate self-identity.

Untouched by memories, thoughts or characteristics,
It is like the water of a mirage.
Unbound and unfreed it does not waver
From its unchanging presence.
All sentient beings are the apparition of mahamudra.
The essence of these apparitions is
All-inclusive space unborn from the very beginning.

All the characteristics of dualistic appearances
Such as happiness and sorrow
Are the play of mahamudra, the innate essence of all phenomena.
This play itself is without truth or permanence.
Although always changing,
It never departs from the seal of empty how-it-is.

B. Presenting the pathway of relative mahamudra

This has two aspects: the deluded pathway and the non-deluded pathway.

First, presenting the deluded pathway

Some cause deep torment by giving empowerments.
Some count on beads saying, "Hung!" "Phat!"
Some ingest faeces, urine, blood, semen and flesh.
Some are deluded by practising the yoga of channels and winds.

second, presenting the non-deluded pathway

This has four aspects.

1. First, instructions on the definitive view

E Ma Ho!

Being guided by a pure guru
Awaken in this way to the one point to be known:
As everything is within delusion, there is no perfect awakening.
As there is nothing to awaken to and no one to do the awakening
It is beyond partiality.
As there is neither freedom nor non-freedom,
This is the state of unchanging equality.
If one truly awakens in this way there is no need to ask others.

As everything is the clarity of the dharmakaya,
The mental activity of rejecting and adopting does not occur.
As there is neither meditation nor non-meditation,
Characterisation cannot stain.

There is no reliance on
Perceived appearances and non-appearances;
With no notion of 'actions' or 'actors' there is nothing to fixate on.
Free of the intellect's hopes and fears all longing is left behind.

If you awaken to the unchanging presence of how-it-is
As shown by your guru,
All your various memories and thoughts
Will dissolve within all-inclusive space.
With consciousness not dwelling on objects
One is free of all longing attachment.
Thus all phenomena are liberated
In the state of uncontrived unchanging presence.

Unattached to anything one is free of stains such as pride.
Devoted and well guided by the holy,
One desists from all mental activity and is without stain or doubt.
With knower and known purified,
The essence of phenomena is directly revealed.

If one has not awakened
To unchanging presence mahamudra, then
Always under the power of duality
One will be attached to everything.
Many kinds of dull obtuse thoughts and ideas
Will arise continuously and
Not resting in the unerring truth
One will wander in samsara.

Attachment and craving for fame,
Praise, possessions, respect, and the
Great understanding arising from study and reflection, and
Having good experiences, accomplishments,
Blessing and power are the signs of the path of contrivance.
The wise do not focus on them for they stain the pure meaning.

Taking such things to be the truth
One falls into the two extremes and then
Revolves in samsara, for this is the root of becoming.
Therefore look for the root of the ground of all
And for the essence of mind however it seems.
By looking one sees that there is nothing and is
Freed from all mental activity and so there is certain liberation.

2. Second, pith instruction on the practice of meditation

'This is ...' cannot be applied
In the space of the empty phenomena of the mind
And so within it there is no duality of meditation
And something to meditate on.
Rest unwaveringly in this state
Without thoughts of existence or non-existence.

Emptiness, unborn, beyond intellect and
Free of extremes – with all such mental creations
You will not settle in the truth of how-it-is but will be far away.

Rest in the state of relaxation
Without estimating whether it is empty or not.
Without resting or not resting
Let your mind free without direction.
Free of the mind that discards or holds on,
Be (as mindless) as a corpse.

Aware of the thusness of how-it-is
You will dwell in this state and
The subtle traces of the characteristics of dualistic appearances
Will quickly vanish.

If you do not abide in the state of awakening
And are distracted by concepts
You will not discard the subtle traces
Of the concepts of dualistic experience.

A person with dim sight
May know that they have an eye disease but
If (in fact) there is no eye disease to be cured
There will be no dim appearances to be cleared away.

To construct an idea about how-it-is,
And to desire meditative experiences and
To meditate having taken the truth of thusness as an object –
These are all mistakes!

3. Third, pith instruction on the pathway of conduct

This has three aspects.

Firstly, the actual conduct

Longing and attachment for favourable situations
Become causes of binding.
All unpleasant and adverse situations are true attainment
Since adverse situations clarify a yogi's experience.
Therefore do not reject negative experiences but,
Knowing thusness, protect that within them.
Cultivating such protection
Is the conduct that brings complete experience and awakening
And is like the whip that urges on a fast horse.

If someone with awakening and good experience
Lacks the friend of conduct,
They are like a person with sight who lacks legs.
Practise the truth of the relaxed ultimate state without attachment.
Without discarding or employing, without attachment,
Without acting or desisting,
This is the supreme conduct of doing whatever pleases you
In your own way.

Secondly, presenting where one can go wrong in conduct

Due to desire and longing
One responds to everything by either blocking or employing.
One strays with erroneous conduct
That is not compatible with one's own nature.

Thirdly, presenting not separating from mahamudra commitments

Even if a person has great confidence
That, in relative terms, they are a buddha,
They should not discard the great accumulation of merit
But rather strive at it with as much power as they have.
Even if samsaric beings have minds free of fear and worry
They should shun even the slightest act of unvirtue.

Even though all phenomena are empty, free of extremes
And pure like space,
You should root out all limiting desire and aversion,
Grasping and clinging.
Even though you have awakened to the truth
Of the great direct limitless essence of all phenomena,
Until you have attained stability
You should keep your experiences and insights
Secret from others.

Even though you have awakened to
The ultimate non-duality of self and other,
Relatively, you should concern yourself with
The great value of benefiting sentient beings.
Even though you have the great confidence
Of not looking to another for guidance,
You should carry your most kind guru
On the crown of your head.

4. Presenting the result of the complete fulfilment mahamudra

This has two aspects.

1. Presenting the situational result

Being free of both an object to be seen and one who sees,
Differentiation is liberated where it is.
Eliminating the one who does the practice,
There is freedom from all striving at accomplishment.
Discarding the result that can be gained,
One is liberated from all hopes and fears.
Having extirpated the ego-self,
One is victorious in battle with the mara demons.
Having destroyed reified entities on the spot,
One is freed from every aspect of samsara and nirvana.

2. Presenting the ultimate result

Awareness has the purity of the ground
Therefore it is known as 'perfect buddha'.
When phenomena and intellect are brought to cessation,
This is called 'nirvana'.
Uncontrived and unchanging
This is complete liberation from discarding and gaining.

C. Thirdly, the immediacy of mahamudra, the inseparability of the two truths

E Ma Ho!
Whatever is named by the profound great sound 'mahamudra',
The basis for this is also named 'empty' as a mere label.
As each moment is inherently empty
Who is there to awaken to selflessness?
With no one to awaken to this,
'Buddha' is merely name, symbol, expression.

These attributions lack truth and are just a beginner's idea.
Such beginners are themselves without self,
Illusory and mere apparitions.
What is called mahamudra
Is just a label used by immature beginners.

Deluded and undeluded are also merely names and labels.
Who is the aware person who experiences delusion?

There is not even a dust particle of the result of nirvana:
It cannot be found.
What are known as liberation and bondage
Are incidental attribution.
How can non-existence be freed or bound in peaceful pure space?
What are called relative and ultimate
Are also names persistently applied:
The all-inclusive space of dharmadhatu
Is free of the two truths and free of all-inclusive space.

This concludes *The Doha Treasury* composed by the powerful Yogi Virupa. The Indian Abbot Sri Vairocana (Rakshita) translated it himself.

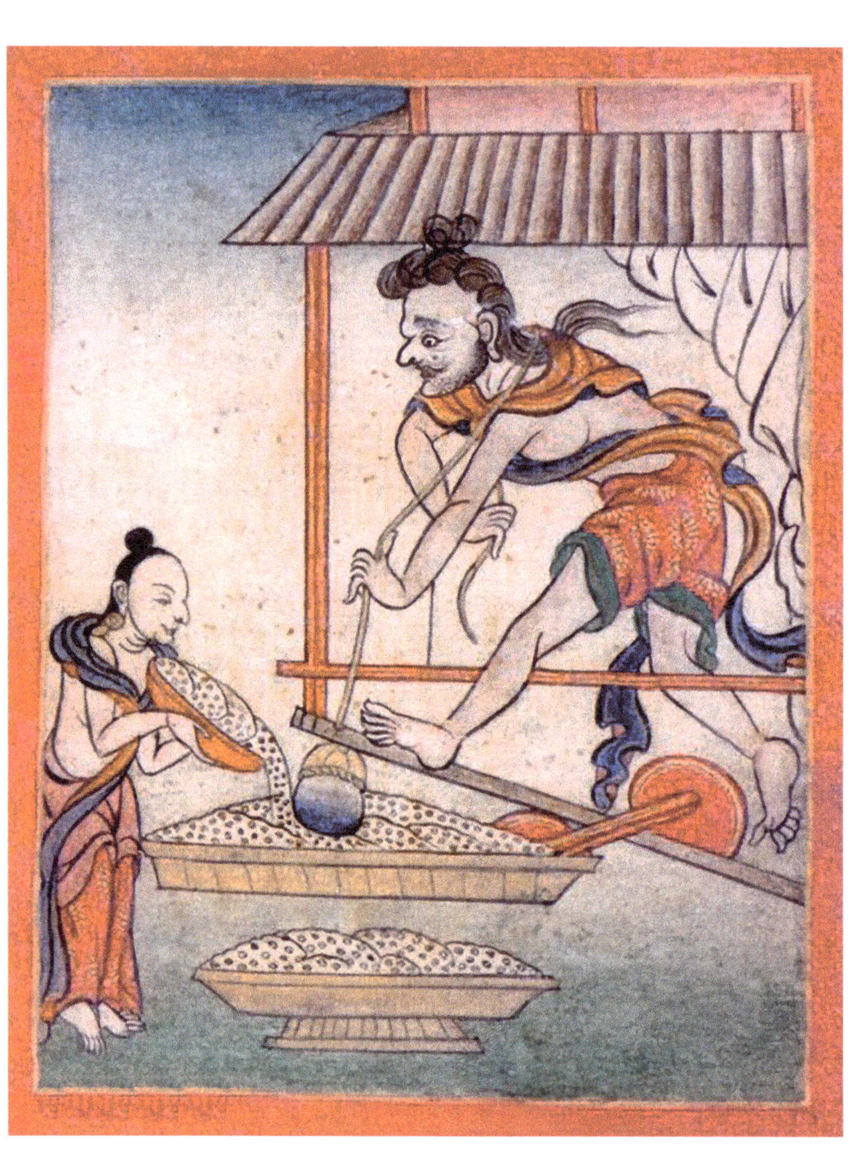

THE DOHA TREASURY OF TILOPA

IN THE LANGUAGE OF INDIA: *DOHAKOSANAMA*

IN THE LANGUAGE OF TIBET: *DO HA MDZOD CES BYA BA*

I pay homage to Sri Vajrasattva!
I pay homage to unchanging intrinsic awareness mahamudra!

This text has two parts: A) the extensive teaching and
B) the brief teaching.

A. THE FIRST PART HAS FOUR SECTIONS

FIRSTLY, PRESENTING THE VIEW

The (five) aggregates, the (eighteen) factors of experience
And the (twelve) aspects of the sense fields –
Without exception they all arise from and dissolve within
The nature of mahamudra.

The substantial and the insubstantial
Are both beyond conceptualisation.
There is nothing for mentation to do
And no meaning to be sought.
As all things are constitutionally false and deceptive
Beginning and ending are discarded.

Whatever becomes an object of consideration for mentation
Is not actually how it is, being a subjective naming.
Actuality is not something made by the guru or by the disciple.

Without taking it to be mind or non-mind,
Know it to be singular and free of the many.
Attachment to the singular is itself the sole binding.

Secondly, presenting the meditation.

I, Tilo, have nothing to teach.
My dwelling is not secluded nor is it not secluded.
My eyes are not open nor are they shut.
My mind is not contrived, nor is it uncontrived.
Know that original presence offers mentation nothing to do.

Actuality is untroubled by conceptual dichotomising, and so
Suddenly occurring experiences, memories, and knowledge
Are to be seen as false and deceptive, and left as they are.
There is nothing at all to value or to devalue, to gain or to lose.

Thirdly, presenting the conduct

Do not strive at austerities in the forest!
You will not find happiness through bathing and ritual purity.
Moreover you will not gain liberation
By making offerings to the gods.
Come to know the idleness free of accepting and rejecting.

Fourthly, presenting the result

This has two aspects:

1. The result according to circumstances

   Awareness of one's intrinsic thusness is the result.
   The moment one awakens to this there is no path to follow.
   Yet the foolish of this world go searching for it elsewhere.
   Cut free from following hopes and fears.
   This is happiness.

2. The final result

   If someone pacifies their mind's grasping at a self,
   The appearances of dualism are completely purified.

B. The second part presents the summary

Without thinking, imagining or diagnostic analysis,
Without meditating or acting or hoping or fearing,
The mental constructs that support such grasping at something
Are liberated where they are
And with this one arrives exactly on the primordial actuality.

This concludes the text entitled *The Doha Treasury* composed by the powerful yogi, Tilopa. It was translated into Tibetan on his own by the Indian abbot Vairocana (Rakshita).

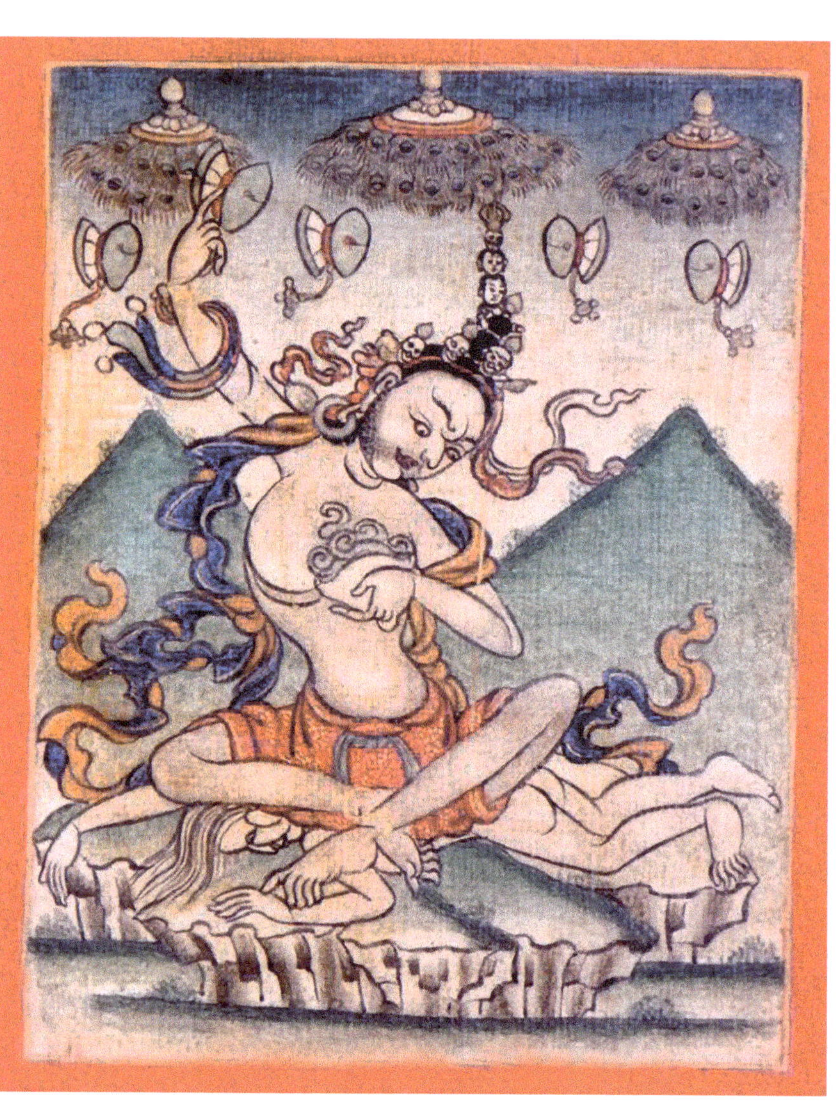

THE DOHA TREASURY OF KRISHNAPA/NAGPOPA

IN THE LANGUAGE OF INDIA: DOHAKOSANAMA

IN THE LANGUAGE OF TIBET: DO HA MDZOD CES BYA BA

I pay homage to the effortlessly presencing original essence!

This text has two parts: A) Ending limitation of the view, meditation, conduct and result

B) the unobstructed incalculable original essence

A. The first part has four sections

Firstly, ending limitation of the view

Worldly beings develop arrogance
On the basis of diverse scriptures and analysis and
Claim to have entered emptiness.
There being no error, there is no entry.

Emptiness is also empty due to emptiness.
Being without birth it does not give rise to birth.
All of that is false.
There is no essence to such going, changing or healing.

Whatever the intellect develops thoughts about
Is mere thought and not true awakening.
Due to this the sickness will return again fully.

Secondly, ending limitation of meditation

Conceptual thought is itself delusion.
The object and its knower are both unreal.
Impermanent and false, they lack truth.
Therefore they are the path of delusion.

When the intellect takes an object
Even the unagitated lord is brought down;
The host of buddhas, worldly goddesses, wrathful deities and
The entirety of the mandala will fully decline.

Thirdly, ending limitation of conduct

It is a mistake to strive for accomplishment.
Adopting and rejecting ends in exhaustion.

Fourthly, ending limitation of result

The essence of all phenomena is like the space.
Those who wish to arrive there
Are like hungry ghosts searching till the end of space.

Those who wish to gain the vital nutrition of the ultimate
Are like deer striving to reach the water seen in a mirage.
As a buddha from the very beginning,
To develop the desire for buddhahood is delusion.

B. The second part: the unobstructed incalculable original essence

Wondrous! An illusory being enters the middle way.
A mountain in the sky is adorned with dream forests.
An elephant appearing in an optical illusion
Strives to reach a mirage river.
The son of a barren woman gains the kingdom of the gandharvas.
However, whatever happens, I, Nagpopa, never change!

The state of original presence is free of the path of effort and striving.
Suchness cannot be fathomed by conceptual thought.
When you see the certain truth
Without calculation and without mistake
You are free of the dualism of empty and not empty.
Phenomena finished, intellect finished – this takes you to the end.

This concludes *The Doha Treasury* of Acharya Krishnapa/Nagpopa. It was translated into Tibetan by the Indian scholar Sri Vairocana (Rakshita) himself.

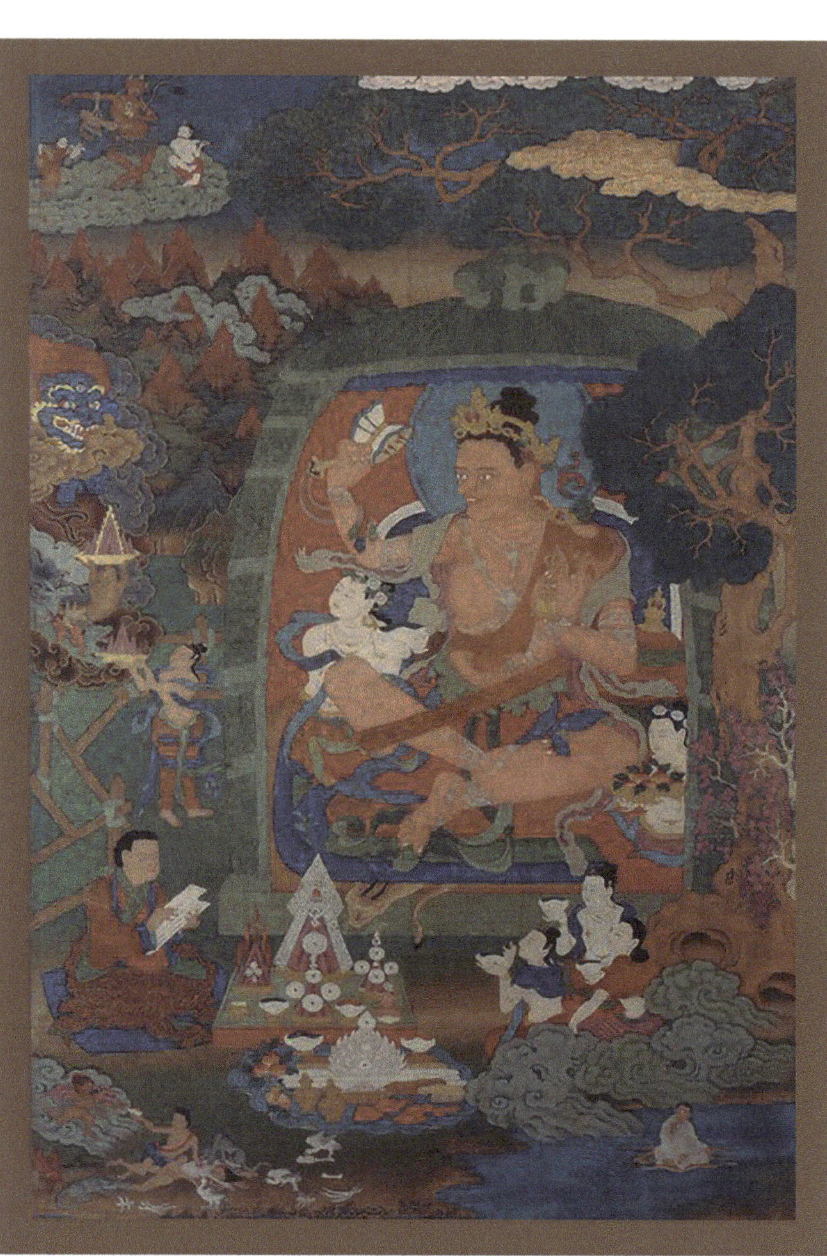

VIEW MEDITATION CONDUCT RESULT
A DOHA SONG
OF
MAITRIPA

IN THE LANGUAGE OF INDIA: BHAVANA DRSHTI CARYA PHALA DOHA GITI NAMA

IN THE LANGUAGE OF TIBET: LTA SGOM SPYOD 'BRAS BU'I DO HA'I GLU ZHES BYA BA

I pay homage to Arya Manjushri

The variety of individual (appearances) is one's own mind.
All (the items that constitute) samsara and nirvana
Cannot be differentiated.
Buddhas and sentient beings cannot be differentiated
Just like water and its waves.

For the awakening yogi of the instantaneous path,
Free of entities and non-entities, the mind itself
Eliminates the dull fog which is the suffering of samsara
Like a small lamp defeating a great darkness.

Mahamudra, the union beyond intellect:
With space-like clarity free of thought
Pervasive vast great compassion
Appears yet without substance like the moon in water.

Clear, free of all notions of edge and centre,
Completely unspoiled, untainted, and free of hopes and fears,
No one knows how to speak of it, like the dream of a dumb person.
Immeasurable great bliss with the nature of discerning wisdom
Is impartial like the light of the sun and the moon.

Wondrous! This self-occurring yoga is amazing!
Uncontrived original mind is the dharmakaya.
The contriving mind will never achieve this yoga
Yet, released from restriction, it will find bliss.

With naturally occurring yoga the intellect is at ease.
Being free of thinking, the desire for peace does not occur.
This is what I, the adept Saraha, say.

Wondrous! In the practice of the view of yoga
My body, this mountain, is the supreme place.
My mind itself, the performer of the yoga of time,
Binds the sense organs, establishes the boundary and
Becomes blissful.

Distracted wavering should not be discarded intentionally,
When encountered, if recognised as your mind, it is your path deity.
Not pulled into knowing,
Involvement in thoughts is gradually abandoned.
When thoughts arise in the mind, the yogi
Remains relaxed and uncontrived like a cotton boll.

Give up activity and let your mind look at itself.
If desire arises, recognise this to be a mara demon.
The root of all thought is your mind, and
As that does not exist, thoughts do not exist.

By meditating, whether there is recollection or not, the yogi
Examines her mind and thus it dissolves into its non-existence.
As there is no desire to meditate,
The result of buddhahood is accomplished.

The yogi is free of thoughts like a small child
Enjoying many flavours like a bee in the garden,
Wandering from forest to forest like a lion,
Always wandering like the ever-changing wind.
If you are heedful of the mind itself, this is the supreme conduct.

Not interrupting one's true nature one behaves like a madman.
This essence of mind, the diversity of appearances –
Merely encountering it reveals the non-existent mahamudra.
The result of buddhahood arises with or without appearances.

When you awaken to this, the best accomplishment,
Outside and inside are the innate itself,
Non-conceptual, like the yoga of a flowing river.
There is nothing to seek other than your own mind.

Non-activity in the mind is the path of mahamudra.
To awaken to the result free of hope is mahamudra.
Thinking about the inconceivable is like a cloud in the sky.
With awakening thusness is naturally empty.

View, meditation, conduct and result are innately inseparable.
To awaken to non-duality is the supreme result of buddhahood.

This concludes *The Doha Song of The View, Meditation Conduct Result* which was spoken by the Indian Abbot, master Maitripa. The very knowledgeable Tibetan translator Mar sTon Chos Kyi bLo Gros (Marpa) translated it.

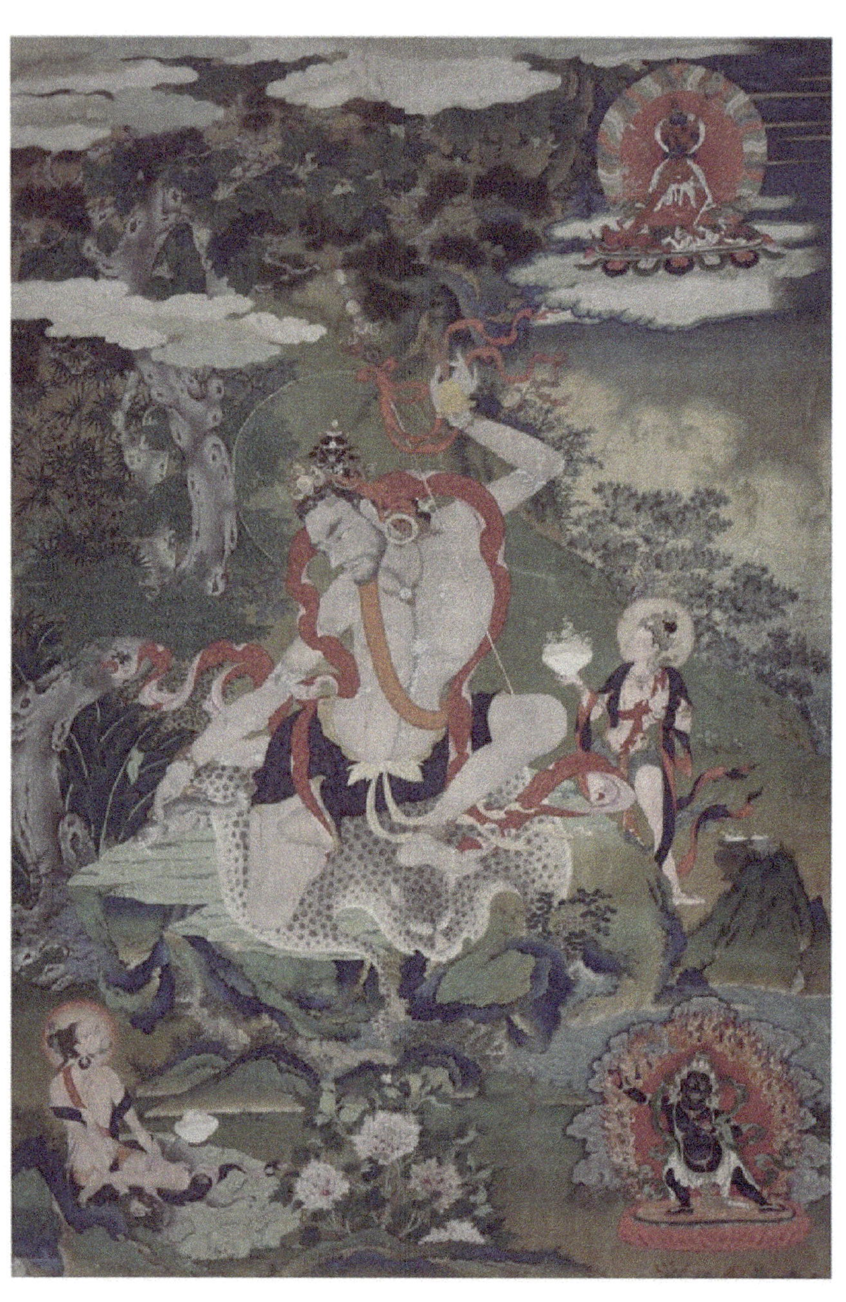

THE GANGES MAHAMUDRA ESSENTIAL INSTRUCTION OF TILOPA

IN THE LANGUAGE OF INDIA: MAHAMŪDRA UPADESHA
IN THE LANGUAGE OF TIBET: PHYAG RGYA CHEN PO'I MAN NGAG

I pay homage to Śri Vajradakini.

With devotion to (me), your guru, you have endured hardship,
Intelligent Naropa, patient in suffering.
You are fortunate so pay attention with your heart. 1

Mahamudra cannot be taught, yet
As an example, in space is there something
that rests on something else?
In the same way in your own mind, mahamudra,
there are no objects to rest on.
Relax at ease in the uncontrived primordial state. 2

If you release your binding your liberation is not in doubt.
For example, by looking at the centre of space seeing ceases.
In the same way if your mind looks at your mind
All thoughts will cease and unsurpassed awakening will occur. 3

For example, both mist rising from the earth and clouds
vanish in vast space
Without going anywhere and without remaining somewhere.
In the same way many thoughts arise in the mind, yet
By seeing your own mind, these waves of thought vanish. 4

For example, space is naturally free of colour and shape.
It is changeless and is not altered by light or dark.
In the same way the essence of your mind transcends
colour and shape.
It is not tainted by the white or black phenomena
of virtue or vice. 5

For example, pure luminosity is the essence of the sun:
The darkness of a thousand aeons cannot dull it.
In the same way the radiant essence of your own mind
Cannot be dulled by aeons of samsara. 6

For example, although the term 'empty' is applied to space
It is impossible to say how space actually is.
In the same way, although the mind is said to be 'clear light'
There is no basis for such conventional terms that assert,
'it exists in this way'. 7

Thus the essence of your mind has always been like space.
There are no phenomena that it does not encompass.
Relinquish all physical activity and rest easily as you are.
With your voice silent, empty sounds are like echoes.

With your mind free of mental activity look into
the dharma of immediacy.
Your body has no substance, like a hollow reed.
Your mind, like the depths of space,
is beyond being an object of thought.
Remain relaxed in this state free of discarding or keeping. 8

If the mind is not made an object you rely on, this is mahamudra.
If you become familiar with this and merge as it,
unsurpassed awakening will occur. 9

The followers of mantra and the paramitas,
The vinaya, the sutras, the pitakas and so on,
Will, due to their individual scriptures and philosophical systems,

Be unable to see the clear light mahamudra.
Due to the arising of desire there is obscuration
so that luminosity is not seen.
The vow to guard against thought, the heart of samaya, is lost. 10

With no mental activity, free of all desire,
(Experience is) self-arising, self-quiescent, like waves of water.
If you do not stray from non-abiding non-referential truth
You will not stray from samaya and will be
like a lamp in the dark. 11

If you are free of all desire and do not abide in the extremes
You will see all the dharma teachings of the three baskets. 12

If you give yourself to this truth you will be freed
from the prison of samsara.
Resting evenly in this truth all unvirtue and obscuration
is burnt up.
This is said to be 'the lamp of the teachings'
Foolish beings uninterested in this truth
Are continually carried away to their demise
by the river of samsara.
These foolish ones suffer unbearably in the lower realms –
how sad!
If you wish liberation from unbearable suffering
then rely on a wise guru
For their blessing will enter your heart and your mind
will be liberated. 13

Khye Ho! These samsaric phenomena, the cause of meaningless suffering,
Are fabricated phenomena lacking their own essence –
so look at the true essence!
To be free of all aspects of subject and object is the king of views.
If there is no distraction, this is the king of meditation.
If there is no deliberate activity, this is the king of activity.
If there is no hope and fear the result will manifest. 14

Never being an observable object the mind's nature is clarity.
With no path to travel you have taken the Buddha's way.
Without having anything to habitually focus on,
unsurpassed awakening occurs. 15

Khye Ma! An excellent understanding of worldly phenomena
Cannot be permanent, being like a dream or an illusion.
The meaning found in dreams and illusions does not exist.
So, sadly disillusioned, abandon worldly activity.

Cut all bonds of attachment and aversion
to country and to those around you.
Stay alone in the forest. Meditate in isolated retreat.
Abide in the state that is free of meditation.
If you attain non-attainment you attain mahamudra.

A tree with trunk, branches and leaves
Has a single root which if cut will cause all its parts to wither.
In the same way, if you cut the root of the mind,
the foliage of samsara will wither. 16

For example, if darkness accumulates over a thousand aeons,
All this darkness can be dispelled by a single lamp.
In the same way the clear light which is your own mind
Will instantly dispel the ignorance, unvirtue and obscuration
gathered over aeons. 17

Khye Ho! The experiences of the intellect will not
let one see the truth beyond intellect.
Experiences arising from activity will not
let one awaken to the truth free of activity.
If you wish to open to the truth free of activity and beyond intellect
Cut the root of your mind and leave awareness naked.

Let the water polluted by thought become clear.
Neither inhibiting nor encouraging appearances,
leave them as they are.

Appearance free of rejecting and adopting is mahamudra.
The ground of all is unborn and so remains clear
of the veil of obscurations and traces.

Avoid pride and calculation - settle in the unborn essence.
Appearances are one's own appearance; they are
mental phenomena which come to nothing.

Complete freedom from extremes is the supreme king of views.
Boundless, deep and vast is the supreme king of meditation.
Free of extremes and bias is the supreme king of conduct.
Free of hopes this self-liberation is the supreme result. 18

At first activity is like water rushing in a gorge.
In the middle it is like the gentle flow of the Ganges.
Finally all waters meet like mother and child.

If those of limited intellect cannot remain in this state
They should work with their breath and nourish awareness.
By means of the many aspects of gazing and mind exploration
They should persevere until they rest in the state of awareness.19

If they rely on a karmamudra, the pristine clarity of bliss-void
will dawn.
The blessings of method and wisdom will merge by
Gently bringing down, holding, reversing and drawing up
again so that
It flows to its places and spreads throughout the body.
If there is no lust and desire the pristine clarity of bliss-void
will dawn. 20

Free of white hairs, with long life increasing like the waxing moon,
Radiant complexion and the strength of a lion,
The common siddhis will be quickly attained and
you will flow towards the supreme. 21

May this instruction on the key points of mahamudra
Dwell in the hearts of fortunate beings! 22

This completes the twenty-three indestructible verses on mahamudra taught on the banks of the River Ganges by the master adept of mahamudra, Sri Tilopa, to the learned and accomplished Kashmiri pandit Naropa after he had accomplished the twelve demanding tasks. Great Naropa then transmitted it to the great king of translators Marpa Chokyi Lodro who translated it and finalised it at Naropa's northern residence of Pullahari. Ithi! May there be virtue! 23

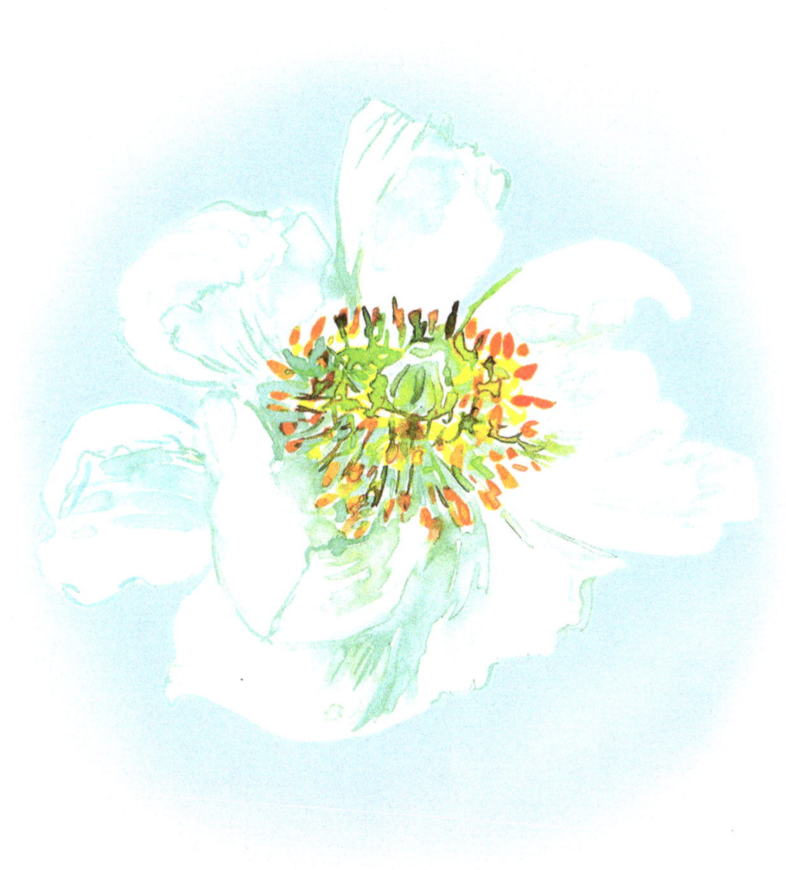

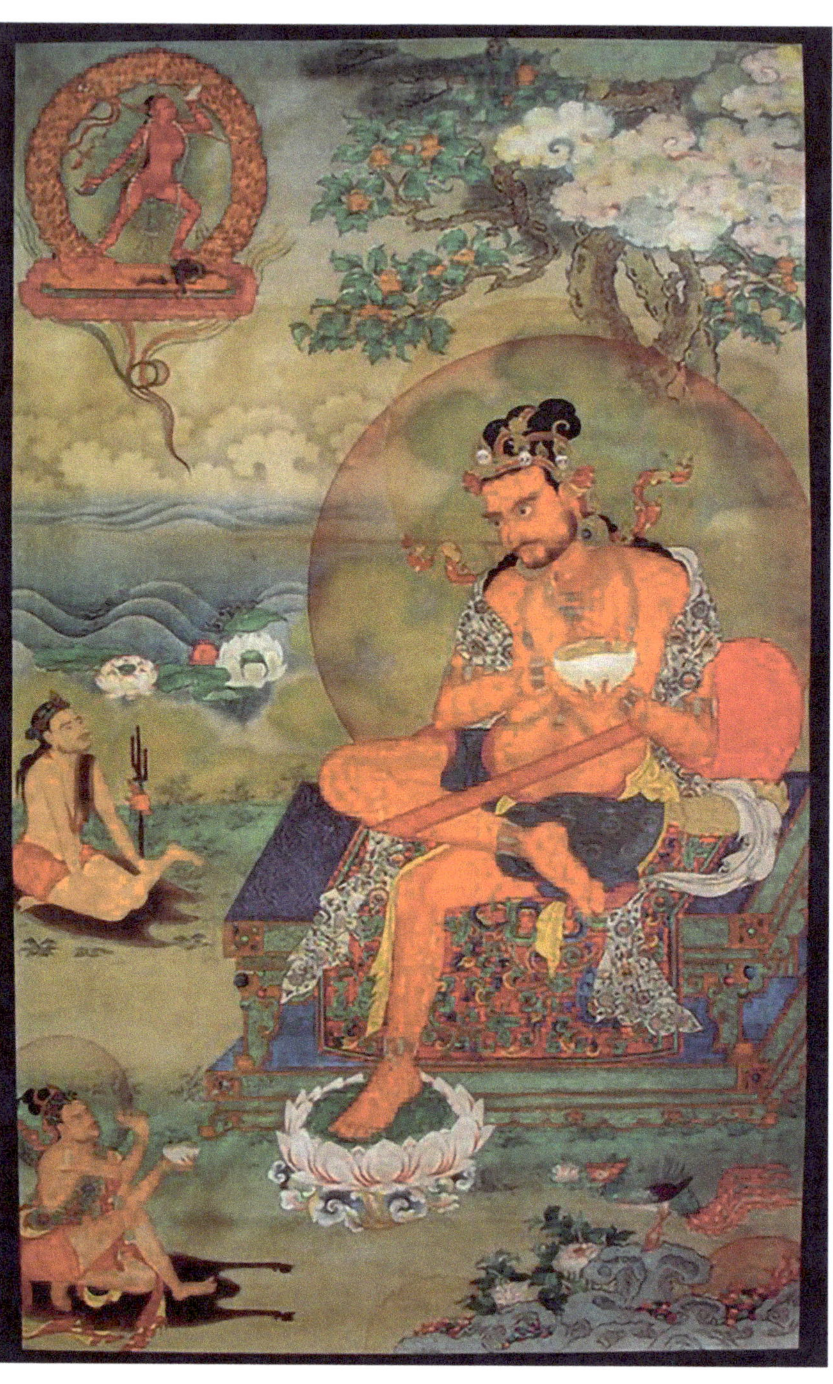

SUMMARY OF THE VIEW BY NAROPA

IN THE LANGUAGE OF INDIA: *ADHI SIDHI SAMA NAMA*

IN THE LANGUAGE OF TIBET: *LTA BA MDOR BSDU PA ZHES BYA BA*

I pay homage to Vajra Dakini.

I pay homage to the omniscient one,
Our principle protector, the benefactor of beings.

Following scripture and reasoning
I will summarise and clarify the true meaning.

The phenomena which appear and which are possible
Are not found apart from your self-aware mind.
Because their appearance is clarity
They are like self-aware experience.

If these appearances were not the mind,
Lacking a connection there would be no appearances.
This is how the relative is made clear.
As it is said, *'Know that all phenomena dwell in the mind.'*

The main practice of dharma is the mind itself.
Yet even with attentive minute analysis,
Whether these two, the naturally luminous mind and
The defilement of incidental thoughts,
Are the same or different,
Is a truly great profundity.
Because it is most profound, scholars analyse it.
Although it is taught, it is not written down.

Emptiness itself is the aware mind.
Bodhicitta is also just this.
The buddha families are also just this.
The buddha nature is just this.

With the taste of exactly this as it is,
Great bliss is also just this.
Secret mantra is also just this.
Method and discerning wisdom is just this.

The profound and vast is just this.
Samantabhadra and consort are just this.
Appearance and emptiness, space and original knowing
Are to be known as primordial buddhahood.

Even with its stains, self-awareness
Does not look to anything else and so
Self-arising original knowing is just this.
This is awareness and so it is clear.

It is self-aware and therefore non-conceptual.
Self-aware, it is not possible for it to think about itself.
Not being an object for thought,
The mind is inconceivable.

Original knowing is clarity free of thought.
It is like the original knowing of the sugatas.
Due to this the mind itself is luminosity.
It is said, *'Seeing that the mind is original knowing*
Do not seek buddhahood elsewhere.'

Nevertheless, that mind, due to incidental
Thought stains, becomes afflicted,
Just as water, gold and space
Are sometimes pure and sometimes impure.
However the mind has the nature of luminosity and

Is free of even a hair-tip of substance.
It is like a lotus in the sky.
In that way existence has no reality, and so
Non-existence also has not the least reality.
Because of their mutual dependence
If this 'side' is unreal so is the other 'side'.

It is not both existent and non-existent
Because each has been refuted separately.
It is not neither existent nor non-existent
Because existence and non-existence are contradictory.
It is not embodied beings and
Neither is it not embodied beings.
Therefore it is beyond all conceptualisation.
This is how the absolute is made clear.
As it is said, *'The mind abides as space.'*

Intrinsically aware beyond conceptualisation
It is empty while appearing and appearing while empty.
Thus it is the inseparability of appearance and emptiness
Like the reflection of the moon in water.
This is how non-duality is made clear.
As it is said, *'Space does not abide anywhere.'*

Intrinsically aware beyond conceptualisation
It is the very basis of samsara.
Nirvana also is just this.
The great middle way is also just this.
What is to be seen is just this.
What is to be meditated on is just this.
What is to be attained is just this.
The valid truth is just this.

Cause, method and result,
Famous as the threefold continuum, and
Ground, path and result,

Are also simply moments of just this.
It is known as the 'root consciousness', as 'the ground of all',
As 'all the possible components of samsara',
As 'dependent' and so forth.

Wondrous! The mind itself and its stains
Emanate the beings of the six realms
In the limitless expanse of space
As inconceivable suffering and delusion.

Free of the stains of thought,
Intrinsically aware beyond conceptualisation,
Is the nirvana which does not abide anywhere.
Vajrasattva is also just this.
The six buddhas are also just this.
The six classes of sentient beings are just this.
The youthful Manjusri is just this.
Vairocana is just this.

Dharmakaya and great bliss and
What is called 'union' are also just this.
The fourth initiation is also just this.
Innate joy is just this.
Intrinsic purity is also just this.

The sutras and tantras give these and
Many other famous descriptive terms.
They are all based on this and
Are used according to requirement.

Wondrous! Stainless mind itself
Emanates form mode aspects including
The completely pure buddha realms and
The emanated illusory mandalas.
These truly amazing emanations
Appear and pervade limitless space.

The ignorant non-buddhist tirthikas
Call their own minds
'Atman' and 'purusha' and
Enter the ocean of erroneous traditions.

Even in our own tradition, the sravakas,
The pratyekabuddhas and the cittamatrins
Maintain the duality of grasping subject and graspable object
While thinking that non-duality is the ultimate.
Moreover those with ideas of 'fully true', 'fully false' and so on
Enter the web of concepts.

By not making such mistakes regarding the view,
Meditation and conduct will be pure and
Harmonious with the actual and
Thus enlightenment will be attained
Like a trained horse winning the race.

If one is not in harmony with the true view
Meditation and conduct become delusion and so
The actual result will not be attained,
Like a blind person without a guide.

The true meaning is deep like the ocean.
How can my intellect which is like a frog in a well
Gain the depths by splashing about?
May the wise ones forgive my errors.

By whatever virtue this work generates
May fortunate and worthy beings
Eliminate their delusional stains
So that the discerning wisdom of awakening is born!

This concludes Naropa's *Summary of the View*. It comes from the mouth of Pandita Jnanasiddhi (Naropa's dharma name). It was requested and translated by the translator Marpa Chokyi Lodro.

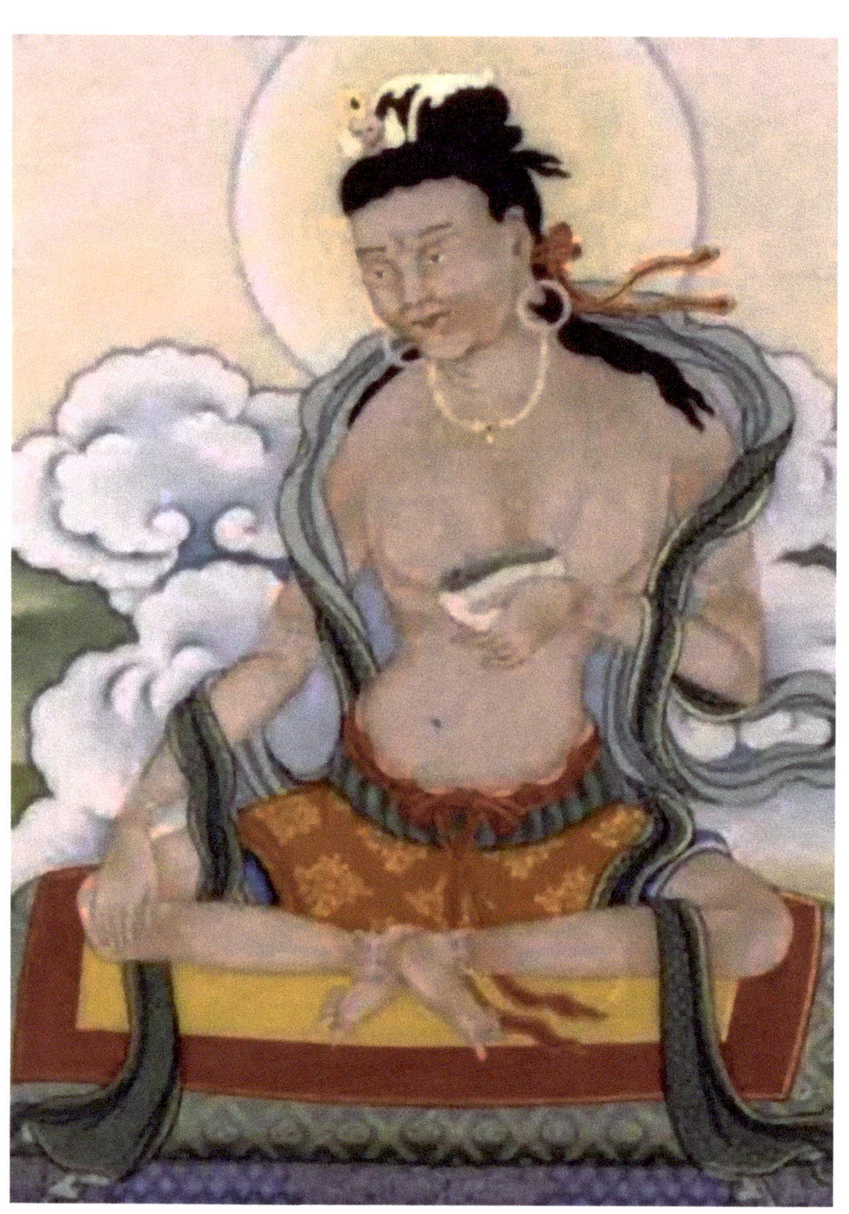

MAHAMUDRA IN A FEW WORDS BY MAITRIPA

IN THE LANGUAGE OF INDIA: SANCAMITHA

IN THE LANGUAGE OF TIBET: PHYAG RGYA CHEN-PO TSHIG BSDUS PA

Paying homage in the state of great bliss
I shall indicate mahamudra.
All phenomena are one's own mind:
Seeing things as being outside is a delusion of the intellect.
Like dreams they are essentially empty.

The mind also is just the movement of memory and ideas:
Lacking inherent existence it is like the energy of the wind,
With its empty essence, it is like the sky.
All phenomena abide in evenness, like the sky
Thus do I indicate what is called 'mahamudra'.

One's own essence cannot be shown.
Hence the true nature of the mind
Does not alter or change
From its actual state of mahamudra.

If someone should truly awaken to thusness
All that appears and exists is mahamudra,
The great all-pervading dharmakaya.
Rest at ease in uncontrived presence.

The dharmakaya cannot be thought about:
Meditate by resting without seeking.
Meditation with seeking is a delusion of the intellect,

Being like the sky or a magical illusion.
Without either meditation or non-meditation
What is there to separate or not separate?
For the yogi who awakens to this
All virtuous and unvirtuous actions
Are liberated by knowing thusness.

The afflictions are great original knowing.
Like fire in the forest they are a yogi's friend.

Who is it who goes or stays?
If you stay in isolation and settle your mind
Yet do not awaken to thusness
You will not be liberated even from circumstances.

If you awaken to thusness what could bind you?
Dwelling undistracted within this state
Body and speech are uncontrived and there is no meditation.
Whether you 'rest in equanimity' or 'do not rest'
There is no need for contrived meditation as an antidote.

Within this everything lacks reality.
Whatever appears should be known to be
Without inherent existence.
Appearances, self-liberating, are the dharmadhatu.
Awakening to self-liberation is the great original knowing.

The dharmakaya, non-dual and equal,
Like the flow of a great river,
Has full value wherever it is.
It is always buddhahood itself.

Great bliss is free of the objects of samsara.
All phenomena each in their particularity
Are empty in their own essence.
The intellect that grasps at emptiness is purified through itself.

Free of the intellect there is nothing for mentation to do.
This is the path of all the buddhas.
For those who become worthy
I have summarised this essential teaching.
Through this may all beings without exception dwell in mahamudra.

This concludes *Mahamudra In Brief* by Maitripa. This teaching was received directly from that sage and translated into Tibetan by Marpa Chokyi Lodro.

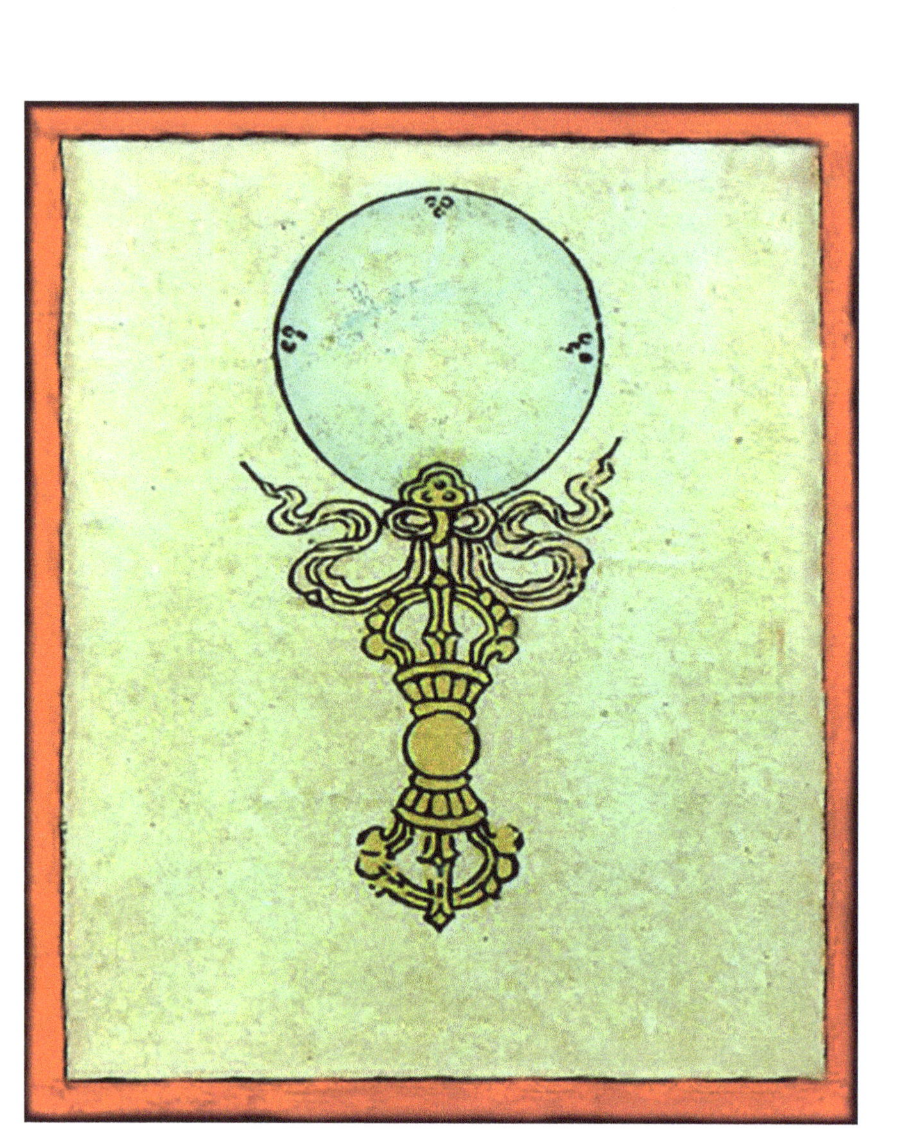

SECTION 2

EXPRESSION OF MAHAMUDRA

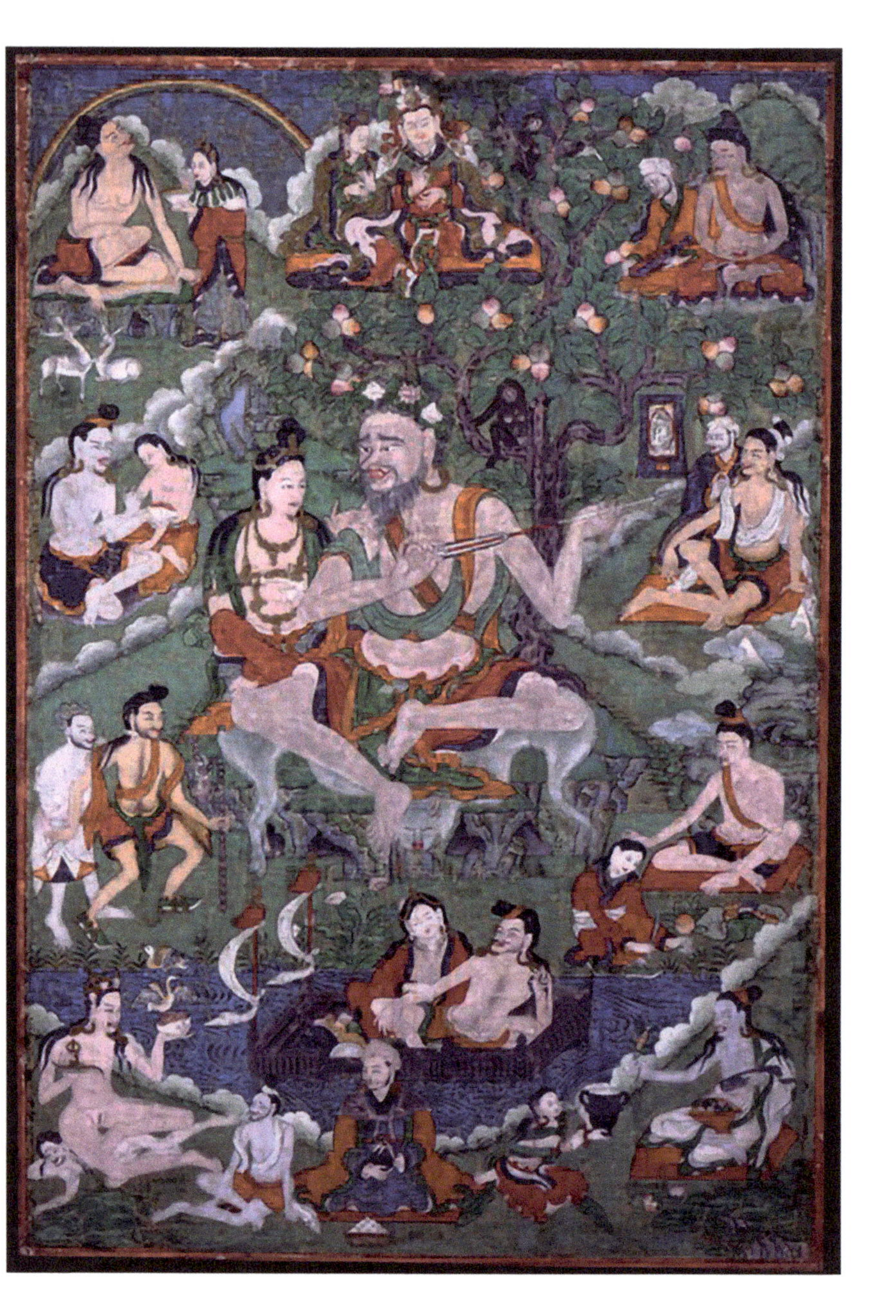

SRI SARAHA
RESPONDS TO THE QUESTIONS OF THE ADEPT MAITRIPA

IN THE LANGUAGE OF INDIA:	*ŚRĪ SARAHA PRABHU MAITRĪ PĀDA PRAŚNOTTARA*
IN THE LANGUAGE OF TIBET:	*DPAL SA RA HA DANG MNGA' BDAG MEE TRI PA'I ZHU*

Homage to the Guru.

All-pervading, all-presenting, yet in no way revealed,
Inconceivably beyond objectification,
Without limits or centre, free of all partiality,
I bow to the primordial complete presence.

The noble great Brahmin Saraha replied to Maitripa
Regarding the ultimate vision of mahamudra.
In order that the yogis who follow me and
Their own faithful followers be benefited,
Without addition or omission I have written here
The profoundly meaningful speech of these Gurus.

The adept bodhisattva Maitripa asked the great brahmin Saraha, *"When it is said that 'mahamudra is everywhere', in what way is this so?"*

"When you understand and awaken to it, this is how it is."

"Is it that 'mu' (Phyag, hand) signifies appearance, 'dra' (rGya, seal) signifies emptiness, and 'maha' (Chenpo, great) is their inseparable union? Appearance and emptiness unified as one – is that what is called mahamudra (Phyag rGya Chen Po)?"

Then Saraha said, *"That is what is known as the mudra of phenomena. Mahamudra is not like that."*

Again a question was posed, *"Well, does 'mu' indicate bliss and 'dra' indicate emptiness and 'maha' their inseparable union so that mahamudra can be said to be bliss and emptiness unified as one?"*

The noble one replied, *"That is the mudra of activity (karma mudra). Mahamudra is not like that."*

"Is it then that 'mu' indicates clarity, 'dra' indicates emptiness and 'maha' indicates their inseparable union so that mahamudra can be said to be clarity and emptiness unified as one?"

The noble one replied, *"That is mudra of light. It is not mahamudra."*

A further question, *"Well, does 'mu' indicate awareness, 'dra' indicate emptiness and 'maha' their inseparable union so that mahamudra can be said to be awareness and emptiness unified as one?"*

The noble one replied, *"That is the mudra of mentation. It is not mahamudra. These are all merely aspects of mahamudra and are only partial. They are not mahamudra itself."*

"Well, please say how mahamudra actually is."

The response was, *"Regarding mahamudra, it does not separate the ground, path and result. It does not keep to the fourfold structure of view, meditation, conduct and result. It is other than the meaning of the fourth initiation. It does not attend to clarity, emptiness and non-thought. It does not rely on the aspects of calm abiding and pure insight. The scholar cannot teach it. The student cannot learn it. From the very beginning all phenomena have been simply as they are. Mahamudra is one way of naming this."*

Maitripa cried out, *"Well, how should I go about understanding this and awakening to it?"*

"The actual path has no stages or ways so do not busy yourself with really entering on a path and really traversing some stages. There is no cause by which one gains enlightenment so do not hope for one. There is no place in samsara into which you can fall so don't worry about this. The essence of the actuality of all phenomena is undifferentiated so do not create divisions. Sit quietly at ease in silence. Simply let be.

Don't employ your intellect in any way. Don't do any kind of meditating with your mind. Don't rely on any kind of object. Don't entangle yourself in anything to do with the mind. Let it be as it has been from the very beginning. Without conceptualising. Completely without conceptual judgement. No objectification. Resting completely without objects of reference.

The words of explanation, the letters of revelation, the symbols of teaching and the meanings which arise during meditation – these are all completely lacking the true meaning. Since it is like this, neither I nor the Buddha can say how it actually is."

Then Maitripa said, *"Well, say what it is like!"*

"It is indicated by the example of space. Its meaning is the mind. It is signified by what arises through the doors of the five senses. If there is no clarity of understanding mount the horse of the sense organs. If there is no bliss it is like the mallow fruit within its unopened sepal. If there is no comprehension this is because the educated knower has been dispensed with."

As an example, at the time of the authentic truth, the sign of this manifests through the eye organ. At the time of the yogic gaze, there is no hesitancy or doubt. At the time of experience, to abide without any of the limitations of the aspects of stable attention, calm abiding, and existence and non-existence is mahamudra. By coming to know these three signs of success in mahamudra, mahamudra will accompany ordinary mind.

Hence, rest in how it actually is. Free of meditation, carefree. Free of effort, relaxed. Free of intention, flowing. Free of concepts, bright. Free of grasping, wide open. Free of support, as it comes. Free of attention, fully released.

Abiding in effortless practice no interruptions occur. The first obstacle of it being uncleanable is due to being unable to meditate[1] *and unable to clean Vajradhara*[2]*. The second fault of not recognising it is due to it being too close. The third is the fault of not recognising it due to it being too deep. The fourth is the fault of not having confidence due to it being too easy. The fifth is the fault of it being incomprehensible because it is too good.*

Moreover, *"No sadness arises from not knowing dharma. Sadness arises from non-action. No sadness arises from the absence of dharma instruction. Sadness arises from not being able to meditate. No sadness arises due to the absence of a cause for gathering the accumulations. Sadness arises from not accumulating"*

Thus the great Brahmin Saraha responded to Maitripa's questions regarding mahamudra. Their words were written down by the pandit Amitavajra.

Notes

1. due to lack of skill on the path
2. due to lack of awakening to the intrinsic

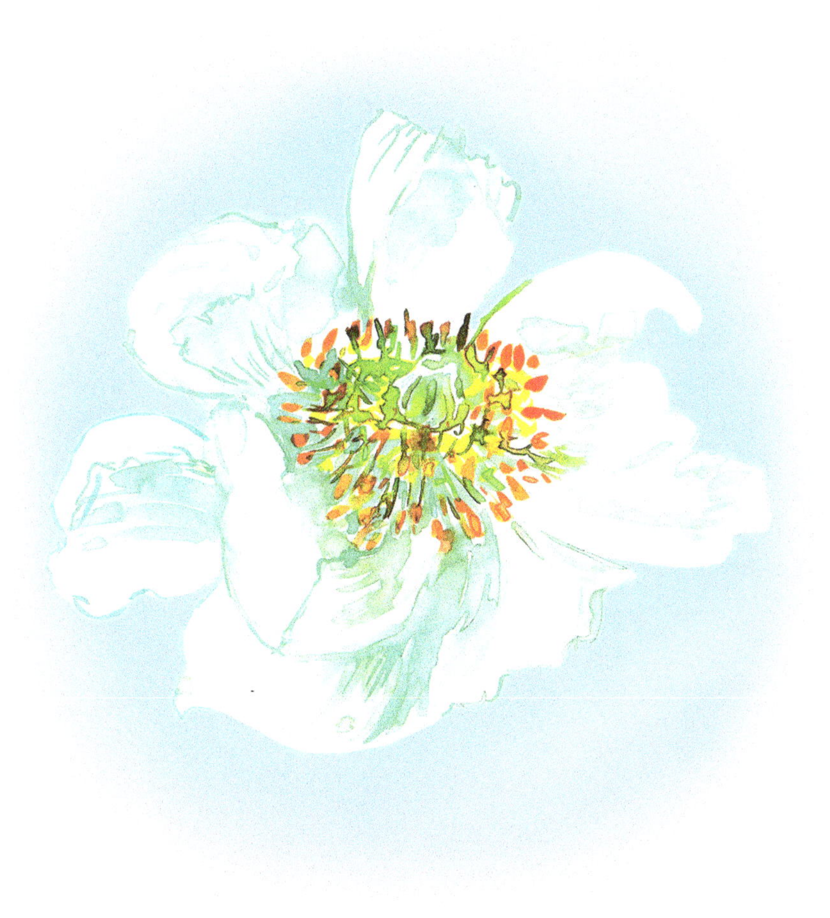

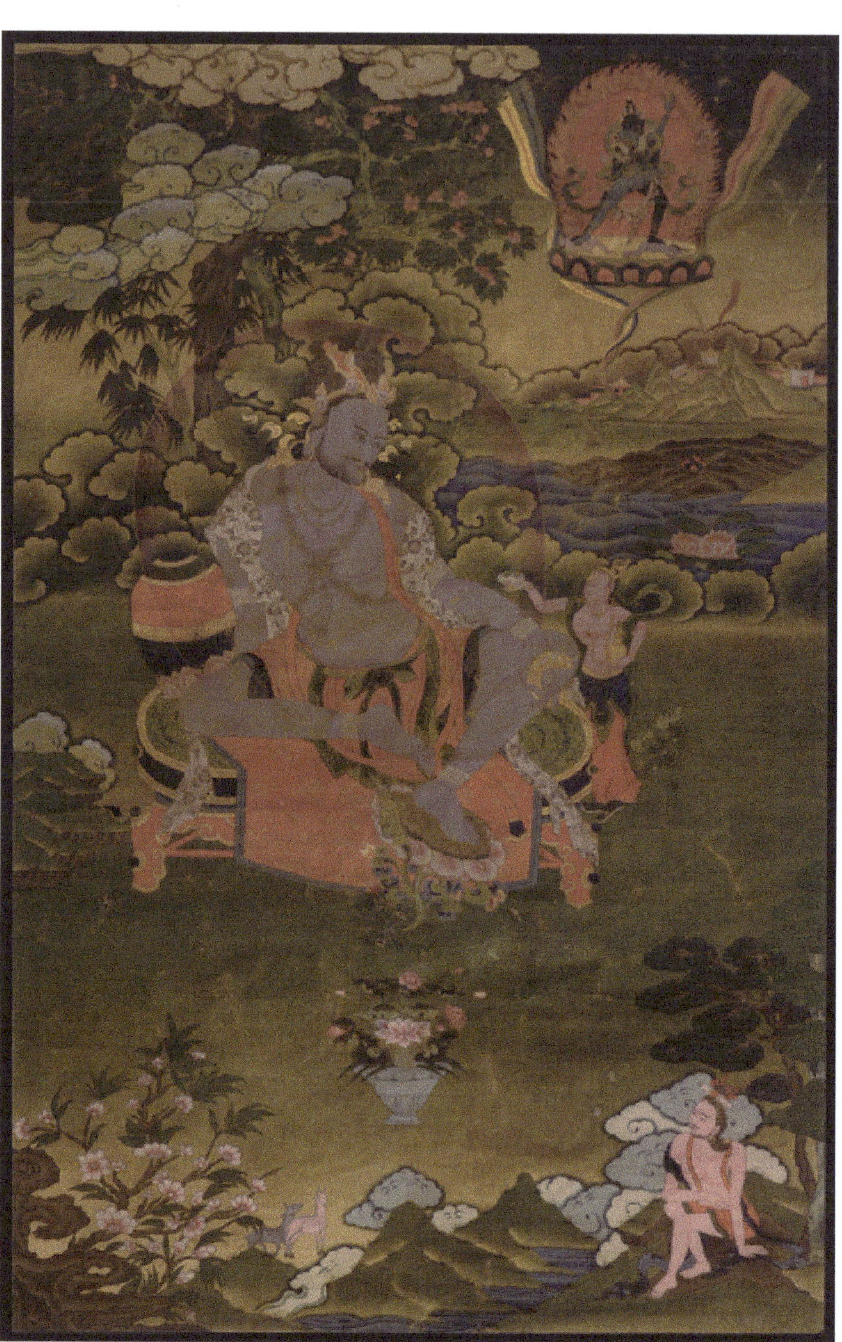

THE GANGES MAHAMUDRA INSTRUCTION GIVEN BY PRECIOUS TILOPA TO NAROPA

[ALTERNATIVE STRUCTURE TO THE VERSION ON PAGE 43]

IN THE LANGUAGE OF INDIA: MAHAMŪDRA UPADESHA

IN THE LANGUAGE OF TIBET: PHYAG RGYA CHEN PO'I MAN NGAG

I pay homage to the Glorious Innate!

Mahamudra cannot be taught, yet as
You have endured hardship with devotion to (me), your guru,
Intelligent Naropa, patient in suffering and fortunate,
Give heartfelt attention to this! 1

Khye Ho! Look well at the phenomena of the world:
Unable to be permanent they are like dreams and illusions.
The truth of dreams and illusions is that they lack existence.
So, disillusioned, give up worldly activity. 2

Reject all the bonds of attractive and aversive involvement with associates and servants.
Meditate alone in forests, mountains and other isolated places.
By abiding in the state of non-meditation
If non-attainment is attained mahamudra is attained. 3

Samsaric phenomena are the cause of meaningless desire
and aversion.
Everything made lacks its own essence
therefore look to the absolute.
The truth beyond intellect will not be seen by relying
on what is available to the intellect.
The uncreated truth will not be reached by anything that is made. 4

If you wish to gain the truth unproduced and beyond intellect,
Cut the root of your mind and leave awareness naked.
Let the water polluted by thoughts become clear.
Neither inhibiting nor encouraging appearances,
leave them as they are.
If you neither adopt nor reject, they are liberated in mahamudra. 5

For example, if a tree with branches and flourishing leaves
Has its roots cut then its many branches and
countless leaves wither.
For example, if darkness accumulates over a thousand aeons,
All this darkness can be dispelled by a single lamp.
In the same way the clear light which is your own mind
Will instantly dispel all the unvirtue and obscurations
accumulated over aeons. 6

If those of limited intellect cannot inhabit this truth,
They should work with their breath and nourish awareness.
By means of the many aspects of gazing and mind exploration
They should persevere until they rest in awareness. 7

For example, if you look carefully at the depths of space,
The apprehension of edge and centre is stopped.
Similarly, if you look carefully at your mind with your mind
The perception of thoughts is stopped
and you rest unreliant on thought.
Then you will see unsurpassed awakened mind as it is. 8

For example, mist rises from the earth forming clouds which
dissolve within the sky's expanse.
They do not go anywhere, nor do they remain somewhere.
Similarly, many thoughts arise from the mind, yet
By seeing your own mind these waves of thoughts dissolve. 9

For example, space is free of colour and shape.
It is changeless and is not tainted by white or black.
Similarly, your own mind is free of colour and shape.
It is not tainted by virtue or vice, nor by anything white or black. 10

For example, pure clarity is the essence of the sun.
It is not dulled by a thousand aeons of darkness.
Similarly the clear light essence of your own mind
Cannot be dulled by aeons of samsara. 11

For example, although the label 'empty' is applied to space
How space actually is cannot be described in such terms.
Similarly, although your mind is said to be clear light,
Such statements of attribution through labelling
are without any actual basis. 12

For example, can space be found to rest on something?
Similarly, your own mind, mahamudra, is free of support.
Rest at ease in the uncontrived primordial state. 13

If your binding is loosened you will have no doubt
about liberation.
Thus the essence of your mind is like space:
There are no phenomena it does not encompass. 14

Release your body from all activity and let it rest at ease.
Saying little let your speech be like an echo.
With your mind free of mental activity
See dharma as it truly is. 15

Like a hollow reed your body has no substance.
Like the depths of space your mind
is beyond being an object of thought.
Remain relaxed in this state free of wandering or settling. 16

When your mind is not relying on a reference point,
this is mahamudra.
By becoming familiar with this through practice,
unsurpassed awakening will occur.
Free of relying on objects the actuality of the mind is clear.
With no path to travel you have taken the Buddha's way.
Keeping to non-meditation unsurpassed awakening occurs. 17

The king of views transcends every aspect of
graspable object and grasping subject.
The king of meditation is free from distraction.
The king of conduct is free of effortful activity.
The result will manifest when you are free of hopes and fears. 18

The unborn source of all is not veiled by
tendencies or obscurations.
Rest in the unborn essence free of the activities
of meditation and post-meditation.
Appearances are self-appearing, exhausting all the phenomena that
the mind knows. 19

The complete liberation from all extremes is the king of views.
Boundless, deep and vast is the supreme king of meditation.
Intrinsic abiding free of activity is the supreme conduct.
Intrinsic abiding free of hopes is the supreme result. 20

At first our activity is like a turbulent river.
In the middle it flows gently like the River Ganges.
At the end the flow meets the ocean
like the meeting of mother and child. 21

The followers of mantra and the paramitas,
Of the dharma in the scriptural collections including the vinaya morality,
And of the philosophical tenets and the various scriptural traditions
Will not thereby be able to see the clear light mahamudra. 22

Not involved in mental activity and free of intention and desire,
Self-arising is self-subsiding
like waves in water.
Due to the arising of desire the clear light is obscured
and not seen. 23

Vows maintained by concepts will stray
from the truth of samaya.
If you do not stray from the non-abiding non-referential
ultimate truth
This perfect practice will be a lamp in the dark.
If you are free of all desires and do not rest in the extremes,
You will see all the dharma contained in the scriptural collections. 24

If you open to this truth you will be freed
from the prison of samsara.
Resting evenly in this truth all unvirtue and obscuration
is burnt up.
This is described as being 'the lamp of the teachings'. 25

Foolish beings uninterested in this truth
Are continuously carried away to their demise
by the river of samsara.
They suffer unbearably in the lower realms - how sad!
If you wish liberation from suffering rely on a wise guru.
By cherishing their blessing your mind will be liberated. 26

If you rely on a karmamudra the bliss-void pristine knowing
will arise
Blessing method and wisdom in union.

Gently bring down, hold, reverse and draw up again
So that it flows to its places and spreads throughout the body.
When there is no clinging to this, bliss-void pristine knowing will dawn. 27

With long life, no white hair, you will wax like the moon, and
Shining with radiant complexion you will possess the strength of a lion.
The ordinary accomplishments will be quickly attained and you will flow towards the supreme. 28

May this instruction on the key points of mahamudra
Abide in the hearts of fortune beings! 29

This concludes what was told to Naropa by Sri Tilopa on the banks of the Ganges. May there be virtue!

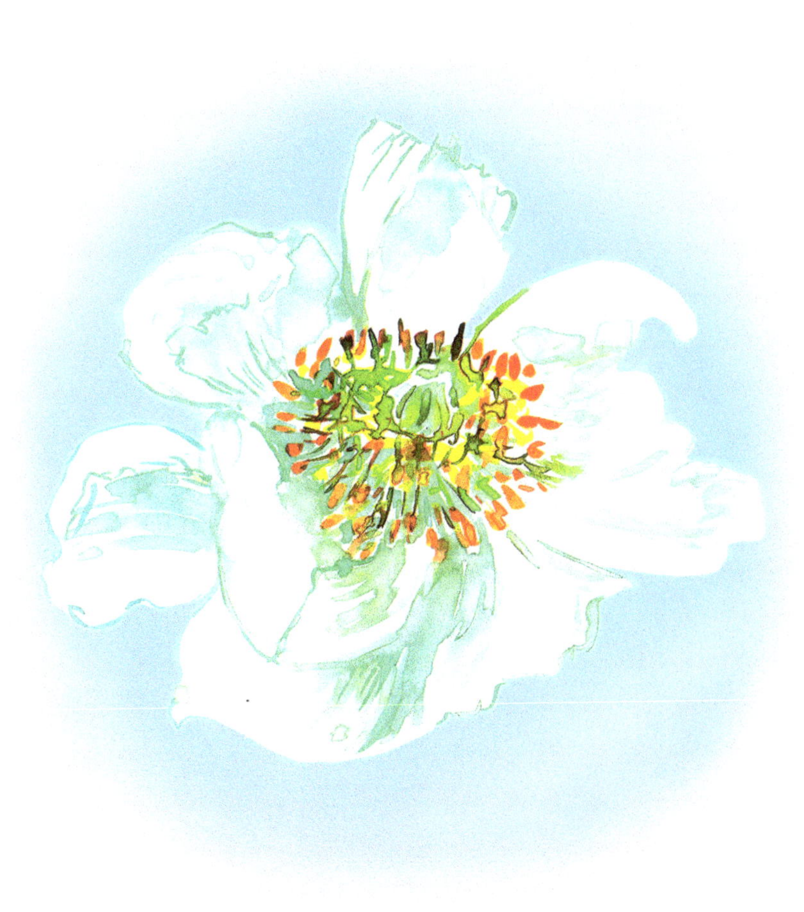

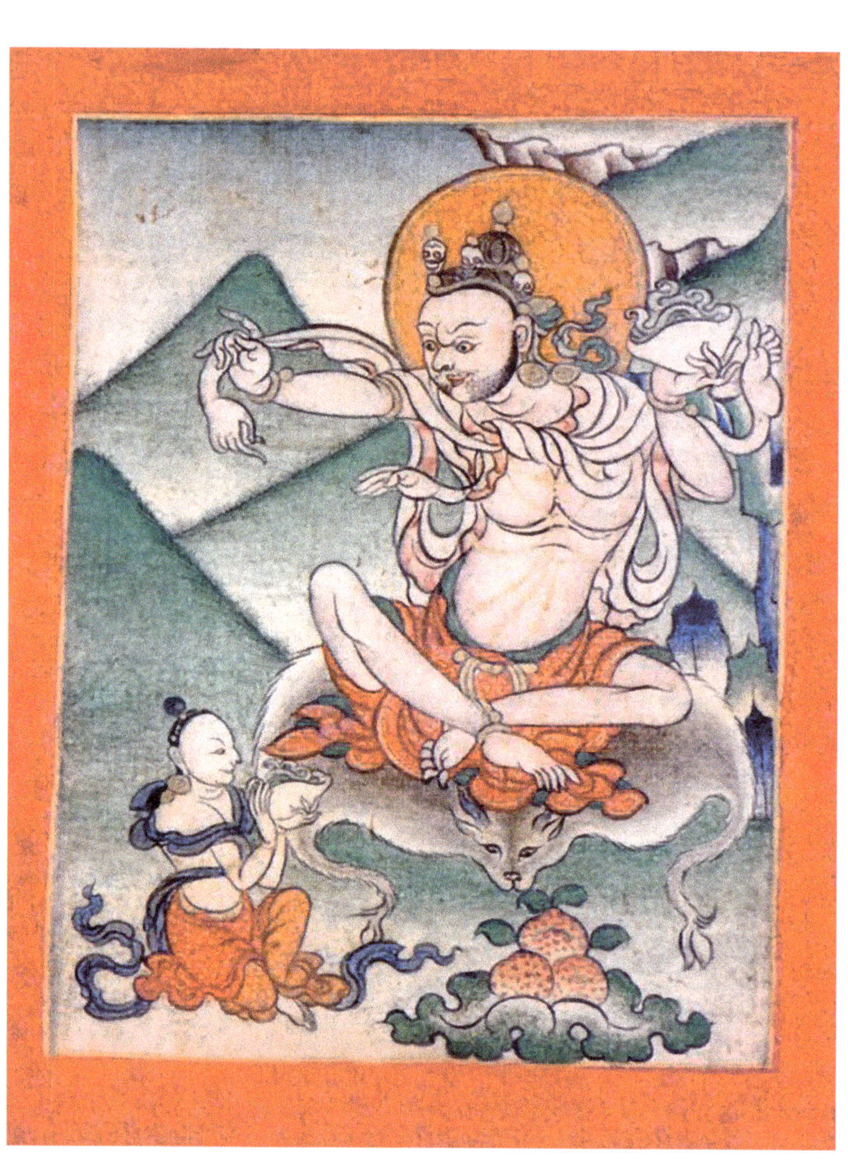

CONCISE WORDS ON MAHAMUDRA FROM NAROPA

In the language of India: Mahāmudrā Saṃcita

In the language of Tibet: Phyag rGya Chen Po Tshig bsDus Pa

I pay homage within the state of great bliss.

Regarding what is called mahamudra
All phenomena are your own mind.
To see meaning as being on the outside is deluded intellect.
As in a dream their essence is empty.

The mind is merely the movement of attention and interest,
Having nothing innate it is like movement of the wind.
Its essence is empty like the sky.
The dharmakaya is like space, being the same everywhere.

Although we speak of 'mahamudra'
Its essence cannot be shown
Hence the actual nature of the mind
Has the nature of mahamudra.

The actual state of mahamudra
Requires neither alteration nor transformation.
If its actuality is seen and one awakens
Then every possible appearance is mahamudra.

The dharmakaya mahamudra is
Innately uncontrived, resting at ease.
The dharmakaya is free of intention:

To stay with this without seeking is meditation.
Meditation involving seeking is deluded intellect.
As with the sky and its magical displays,
Since there is neither meditation nor non-meditation
How could there be separation or non separation?

For the yogi who appreciate this,
All virtues and harmful actions
Will be liberated by just this appreciation.
Afflictions, the great original knowing,
Are a yogi's friend like a fire in the forest.

Why be concerned with going or staying?
Even if you go to a hermitage to gain deep calm
If the actual is not awakened to how will you be liberated?
Temporary situations lack the power to bring liberation.

If you awaken to actuality what can bind you?
Abide in this state without distraction,
Remain free of meditation involving artifice of body and speech
Whether resting or not resting in evenness.

Nothing is established in this state for
Appearances are self-liberating in the dharmadhatu.
Self-liberating thoughts are the great original knowing,
The non-dual ever-even dharmakaya.

Like the steady flow of a great river
However you live will have true meaning.
This is unchanging buddhahood,
This is great bliss, free of anything of samsara.

All phenomena are empty each as they are.
The intellect that grasps at emptiness is pure as it is.
Free of the intellect mentation has nothing to do.
This is the path of all the buddhas.

For those who are truly fortunate
I give this heart instruction in a few words.
By means of this, may all beings without exception
Abide in mahamudra.

This concludes the oral teaching in a few words.

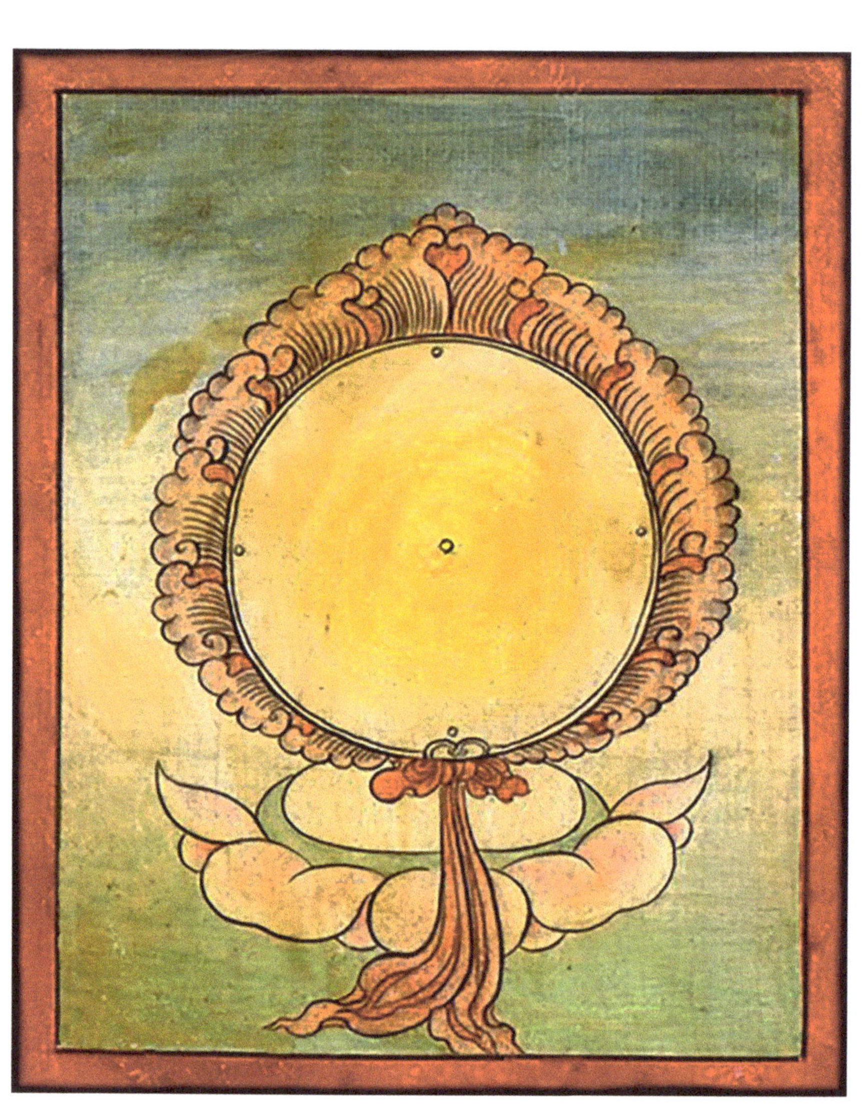

SECTION 3

MAHAMUDRA ASPIRATION

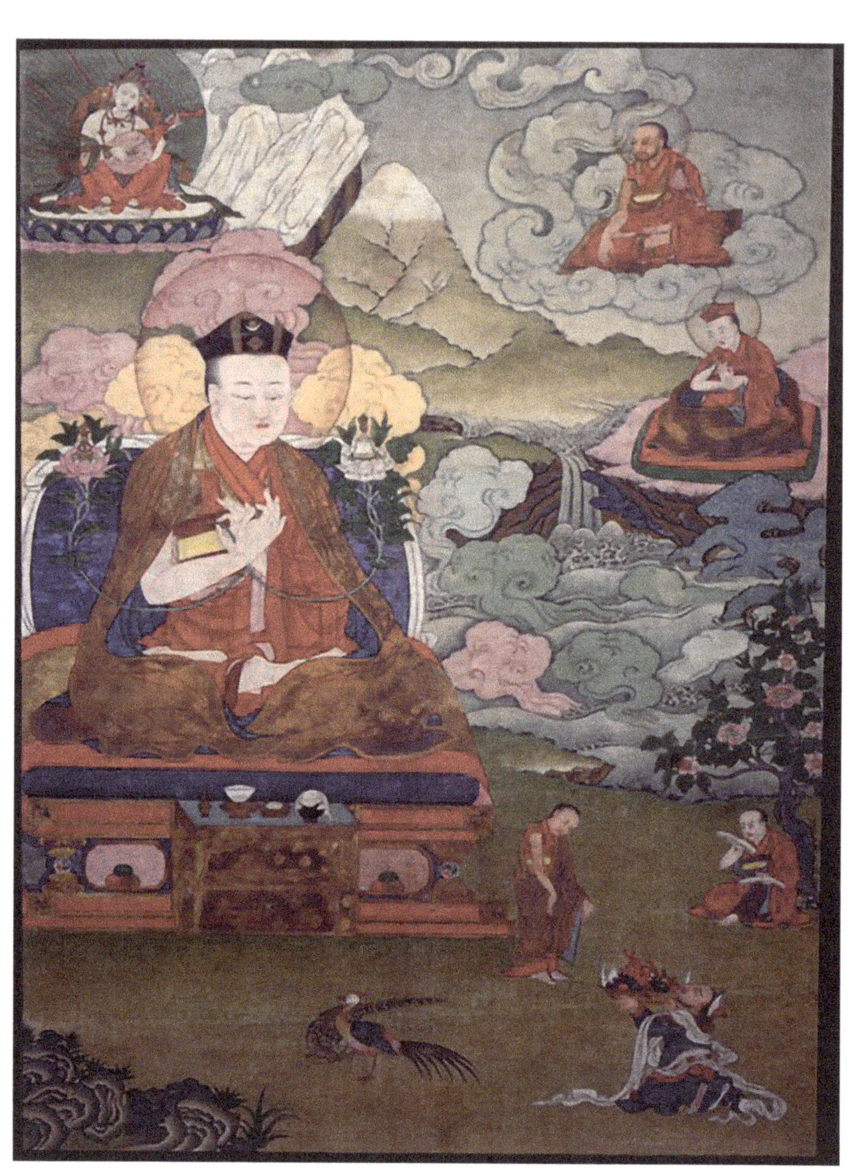

།རྗེ་རང་བྱུང་རྡོ་རྗེས་མཛད་པའི་ངེས་དོན་ཕྱག་རྒྱ་ཆེན་པོའི་སྨོན་ལམ་བཞུགས་སོ།།

ASPIRING FOR THE TRUTH OF MAHAMUDRA BY RANGJUNG DORJE

།ན་མོ་གུ་རུ།

NAMO	**GURU**
homage	*teacher*

Homage to my Gurus.

།བླ་མ་རྣམས་དང་ཡི་དམ་དཀྱིལ་འཁོར་ལྷ།

LAMA MA	**NAM**	**DANG**	**YI DAM**	**KYIL KHOR**	**LHA**
guru, teacher	*plural*	*and*	*reliance or path deity*	*mandala, circle, palace*	*deities*

Gurus, reliance deities, mandala deities,

།ཕྱོགས་བཅུ་དུས་གསུམ་རྒྱལ་བ་སྲས་དང་བཅས།

CHO	**CHU**	**DU**	**SUM**	**GYAL WA**	**SAE**	**DANG CHE**
directions, everywhere	*ten*	*times*	*three*	*jinas, victors, buddhas*	*sons, bodhisattvas*	*together*
		always				

Together with all the buddhas of the ten directions and the three times and their offspring, the bodhisattvas,

།བདག་ལ་བརྩེར་དགོངས་བདག་གི་སྨོན་ལམ་རྣམས།

DA	**LA**	**TSER**	**GONG**	**DA GI**	**MON LAM**	**NAM**
me	*to*	*affection, loving compassion*	*consider, think*	*my*	*aspiration*	*plural*

Please regard us with affection. May these aspirations,

།ཇི་བཞིན་འགྲུབ་པའི་མཐུན་འགྱུར་བྱིན་རློབས་མཛོད།

JI ZHIN	**DRU PAI**	**THUN GYUR**	**JIN LO**	**DZO**
as they are	*made*	*facilitate, conducive*	*bless, inspire*	*do*

With your supportive blessings, be fulfilled in every detail.

Gurus, reliance deities, mandala deities, and
Victors and bodhisattvas of every time and place
Please regard us with affection and bless us
With the fulfilment of these, our aspirations!

།བདག་དང་མཐའ་ཡས་སེམས་ཅན་ཐམས་ཅད་ཀྱི།

DA	**DANG**	**THA YAE**	**SEM CHEN**	**THAM CHE**	**KYI**
I	*and*	*limitless*	*sentient beings*	*all*	*of*

I and all limitless sentient beings

།བསམ་སྦྱོར་རྣམ་དག་གངས་རི་ལས་སྐྱེས་པའི།

SAM	**JOR**	**NAM**	**DA**	**GANG**	**RI**	**LAE**	**KYE PAI**
thoughts	*actions*	*completely*	*pure*	*snow*	*mountain*	*from*	*arising*

Generate snow mountains of very pure intentions and actions

།འཁོར་གསུམ་རྙོག་མེད་དགེ་ཚོགས་ཆུ་རྒྱུན་རྣམས།

KHOR	**SUM**	**NYO**	**ME**	**GE**	**TSHO**	**CHU GYUN**	**NAM**
circles	*three**	*trouble, mess*	*without*	*virtue*	*mass*	*flow, stream*	*plural*

*actor, action, object of action

From which flow streams of virtue free of the muddying three concepts.

།རྒྱལ་བ་སྐུ་བཞིའི་རྒྱ་མཚོར་འཇུག་གྱུར་ཅིག།

GYAL WA	**KU**	**ZHI**	**GYAM TSHOR**	**JU**	**GYUR CHI**
jina, victor, buddha	*body, mode*	*four**	*ocean*	*enter*	*may*

*dharmakaya, open mode; sambhogakaya, radiant mode; nirmanakaya, manifest mode; svabhavikakaya, integrated mode)

May they merge in the ocean of the buddha's four modes.

I and all sentient beings without limit
Generate snow mountains of pure intention and action from which
Flow streams of virtue unsullied by the three concerns.
May they merge in the ocean of the buddha's four modes!

།ཇི་སྲིད་དེ་མ་ཐོབ་པ་དེ་སྲིད་དུ།

JI SI	DE	MA	THO PA	DE	SI DU
up until, for as long as	*that*	*not*	*obtained*	*that*	*until, becoming*

For as long as this is not achieved,

།སྐྱེ་དང་སྐྱེ་བ་ཚེ་རབས་ཀུན་ཏུ་ཡང་།

KYE	DANG	KYE WA	TSHE RAB	KUN TU	YANG
birth	*and*	*birth*	*lifetime*	*all*	*also, until*

In birth after birth, in each and every lifetime

།སྡིག་དང་སྡུག་བསྔལ་སྒྲ་ཡང་མི་གྲགས་ཤིང་།

DI	DANG	DU NGAL	DRA	YANG	MI	DRA SHING
unvirtue	*and*	*suffering*	*sound*	*also*	*not*	*heard, sounded*

May even the words 'harm' and 'suffering' be unheard and

།བདེ་དགེ་རྒྱ་མཚོའི་དཔལ་ལ་སྤྱོད་པར་ཤོག།

DE	GE	GYAM TSHOI	PAL	LA	CHO PAR	SHO
happiness	*virtue*	*ocean's*	*glory, goodness, shining*	*in*	*practice, enjoy*	*may*

May we enjoy wellbeing within an ocean of happiness and virtue.

For as long as this is still to be achieved,
In birth after birth, in each and every lifetime,
Not even hearing the words 'harm' and 'suffering',
May we thrive in the glorious ocean of happiness and virtue!

།དལ་འབྱོར་མཆོག་ཐོབ་དད་བརྩོན་ཤེས་རབ་ལྡན།

DAL JOR	CHO	THO	DAE	TSON	SHE RAB	DEN
precious human life able to practise dharma	*best*	*gained*	*faith*	*diligence, energy*	*wisdom, discernment*	*having*

Having gained the precious freedoms and resources, and endowed with faith, diligence and discernment

།བཤེས་གཉེན་བཟང་བསྟེན་གདམས་པའི་བཅུད་ཐོབ་ནས།

SHE NYEN	ZANG	TEN	DAM PAI	CHU	THO	NAE
spiritual friend, teacher	*good*	*rely on, attend to*	*instruction*	*essence*	*gain*	*then*

May we rely on excellent spiritual friends and receive the essential instructions.

།ཚུལ་བཞིན་སྒྲུབ་ལ་བར་ཆད་མ་མཆིས་པར།

TSHUL	ZHIN	DRU	LA	BAR CHE	MA CHI PAR
manner, current way	*according*	*practise*	*with*	*obstacles*	*not occurring*

Then practising in the proper way without encountering obstacles

།ཚེ་རབས་ཀུན་ཏུ་དམ་ཆོས་སྤྱོད་པར་ཤོག།

TSHE RAB	KUN	TU	DAM	CHO	CHO PAR	SHO
lifetimes	*all*	*in*	*pure, holy*	*dharma*	*practise, use, enjoy*	*may*

May we practise the pure dharma in all our lives.

With the precious freedoms and resources, and
Endowed with faith, diligence and discernment,
May we rely on excellent spiritual friends and
Receive their essential instructions.
Practising correctly without hindrance
May we be true to the pure dharma in all our lives!

།ལུང་རིགས་ཐོས་པས་མི་ཤེས་སྒྲིབ་ལས་གྲོལ།

LUNG RIG	**THO PAE**	**MI**	**SHE**	**DRIB**	**LAE**	**DROL**
instructions, scriptures	*by listening to, studying*	*not*	*knowing*	*obscuration*	*from*	*freed*

Studying the teachings frees us from the veils of ignorance.

།མན་ངག་བསམ་པས་ཐེ་ཚོམ་མུན་ནག་བཅོམ།

MAN NGA	**SAM PAE**	**THE TSHOM**	**MUN NA**	**CHOM**
experience-based teaching	*by thinking about*	*doubts*	*darkness*	*destroy, overcome*

Reflecting on the pith instructions defeats the darkness of doubt.

།སྒོམ་བྱུང་འོད་ཀྱིས་གནས་ལུགས་ཇི་བཞིན་གསལ།

GOM	**JUNG**	**OE**	**KYI**	**NAE LU**	**JI ZHIN**	**SAL**
meditation	*arising from*	*light*	*by*	*how it is*	*as it is*	*clear*

The light arising from meditation clarifies precisely how we are.

།ཤེས་རབ་གསུམ་གྱི་སྣང་བ་རྒྱས་པར་ཤོག།

SHE RAB	**SUM**	**GYI**	**NANG WA**	**GYE PAR**	**SHO**
wise discernment	*three**	*of*	*illumination*	*spread, pervade*	*may*

*study, reflection, meditation

May the illumination of these three aspects of discernment spread everywhere.

Studying the teachings frees us from the veils of ignorance.
Reflecting on the pith instructions removes the darkness of doubt.
The light of meditation clarifies exactly how we are.
May illumination from these three wisdoms spread everywhere!

།རྟག་ཆད་མཐའ་བྲལ་བདེན་གཉིས་གཞི་ཡི་དོན།

TAG	CHE	THA	DRAL	DEN	NYI	ZHI	YI	DON
permanence, eternalism	*nihilism, oblivion*	*limit*	*free of*	*truth*	*two*	*ground, base*	*of*	*meaning, truth, nature*
(all extreme views)				*(relative and absolute)*				

The nature of our ground is the two truths free of the extremes of eternalism and oblivion.

།སྒྲོ་སྐུར་མཐའ་བྲལ་ཚོགས་གཉིས་ལམ་མཆོག་གིས།

DRO	KUR	THA	DRAL	TSHO	NYI	LAM	CHO	GI
exaggeration, adding to, assertion	*depreciation, taking away from, denial*	*limit, edge*	*free of*	*accumulation (of merit and wisdom)*	*two*	*path*	*excellent,*	*by*

With the supreme path of the two accumulations free of the extremes of assertion and denial

།སྲིད་ཞིའི་མཐའ་བྲལ་དོན་གཉིས་འབྲས་ཐོབ་པའི།

SI	ZHI	THA	DRAL	DON	NYI	DRAE	THO PAI
busy samsara	*peaceful nirvana*	*limit*	*free of*	*benefit*	*two*	*fruit, result*	*gain*
				(of self and others)			

There is the result of the two benefits free of the extremes of busy samsara and peaceful nirvana.

།གོལ་འཁྲུལ་མེད་པའི་ཆོས་དང་འཕྲད་པར་ཤོག།

GOL	CHU	ME PAI	CHO	DANG	TRAE PAR	SHO
error, deviation	*mistake*	*without*	*dharma*	*with*	*meet*	*may*

May we meet this dharma free of error and mistakes.

The two truths free of always and never is the nature of the base.
The two accumulations free of assertion and denial is the supreme path
Ensuring the dual benefit free of samsara and nirvana as the result.
May we meet this dharma that does not err or mislead!

།སྦྱང་གཞི་སེམས་ཉིད་གསལ་སྟོང་ཟུང་འཇུག་ལ།

JANG	**ZHI**	**SEM NYI**	**SAL**	**TONG**	**ZUNG JU**	**LA**
purification	*ground, basis*	*mind itself, awareness*	*clarity, luminosity*	*emptiness*	*union, indivisible*	*with, on*

The basis of purification is the mind itself, the union of luminosity and emptiness.

།སྦྱོང་བྱེད་ཕྱག་ཆེན་རྡོ་རྗེའི་རྣལ་འབྱོར་ཆེས།

JONG JE	**CHAG CHEN**	**DOR JEI**	**NAL JOR**	**CHE**
purifying, means, agent	*mahamudra*	*vajra, indestructible*	*yoga*	*great*

That which purifies is the great indestructible yoga of mahamudra.

།སྦྱང་བྱ་གློ་བུར་འཁྲུལ་པའི་དྲི་མ་རྣམས།

JANG	**JA**	**LO BUR**	**THRUL PAI**	**DRI MA NAM**
to be purified	*object*	*suddenly occurring, fleeting*	*delusion*	*stains, marks*

The object of purification is the stain of suddenly occurring delusion.

།སྦྱངས་འབྲས་དྲི་བྲལ་ཆོས་སྐུ་མངོན་གྱུར་ཤོག།

JANG	**DRAE**	**DRI**	**DRAL**	**CHO KU**	**NGON GYUR**	**SHO**
purification	*result*	*stain*	*free of*	*open mode, dharmakaya*	*manifest*	*may*

May the result of purity, the stainless open mode, manifest fully.

The basis of purification is the mind itself,
Luminosity and emptiness inseparable.
The purifier is the great indestructible yoga of mahamudra.
The object of purification is the stain of sudden delusion.
May the result of purity, the stainless open mode, manifest fully!

།གཞི་ལ་སྒྲོ་འདོགས་ཆོད་པ་ལྟ་བའི་གདེངས།

ZHI	LA	DRO DO	CHO PA	TA WAI	DENG
ground, basis	*towards, on, at*	*doubts, elaboration*	*cut, resolve*	*view*	*confidence, conviction*

Cutting all doubts as to the ground is the confidence of the view.

།དེ་ལ་མ་ཡེངས་སྐྱོང་བ་སྒོམ་པའི་གནད།

DE	LA	MA YENG	KYONG WA	GOM PAI	NAE
that	*to*	*unwaveringly*	*protecting, sustaining*	*meditations*	*essential point*

Maintaining this without wavering is the key point of meditation.

།སྒོམ་དོན་ཀུན་ལ་རྩལ་སྦྱོང་སྤྱོད་པའི་མཆོག།

GOM	DON	KUN	LA	TSAL JONG	CHO PAI	CHO
meditation	*meaning, truth*	*all*	*to*	*skilled, expertise*	*conduct, cultivation*	*supreme finest*

Skilfully employing the truth of meditation in all situations is the finest conduct.

།ལྟ་སྒོམ་སྤྱོད་པའི་གདེང་དང་ལྡན་པར་ཤོག།

TA	GOM	CHO PAI	DENG DANG	DEN PAR	SHO
view	*meditation*	*conduct*	*confident*	*have*	*may*

May we have confidence in this view, meditation and conduct.

Cutting away all doubts as to the ground is the confidence of the view.
Maintaining this without distraction is the key point of meditation.
Always skilfully employing meditation's clarity is the supreme conduct.
May we live in the confidence of view, meditation and conduct!

།ཆོས་རྣམས་ཐམས་ཅད་སེམས་ཀྱི་རྣམ་འཕྲུལ་ཏེ།

CHO NAM	THAM CHE	SEM	KYI	NAM TRUL	TE
dharmas, phenomena	*all*	*mind*	*of*	*deluding fabrications, apparitions*	*hence, yet*

All phenomena are apparitions of the mind and

།སེམས་ཉི་སེམས་མེད་སེམས་ཀྱི་ངོ་བོ་སྟོང་།

SEM	NI	SEM	ME	SEM	KYI	NGO WO	TONG
mind	*this*	*mind*	*without*	*mind*	*of*	*nature, essence*	*empty*

This mind is no truly existing mind for mind's essence is empty.

།སྟོང་ཞིང་མ་འགགས་ཅིར་ཡང་སྣང་བ་སྟེ།

TONG ZHING	MA GA	CHIR YANG	NANG WA	TE
empty as it is	*ceaseless, unobstructed*	*whatever arises*	*appears, light*	*hence*

Though it is empty, appearances occur without obstruction.

།ལེགས་པར་བརྟགས་ནས་གཞི་རྩ་ཆོད་པར་ཤོག།

LEG PAR	TAG	NE	ZHI	TSA	CHO PAR	SHO
well, fully	*analyse, investigate*	*then*	*ground*	*root*	*cut, eliminate, determine*	*may*

Fully investigating this may we cut off the source of the reified ground.

All phenomena are the illusory display of our mind.
As for this mind, there is no mind, for mind is empty of essence.
Though it is empty there is ceaseless appearance of all kinds.
May thorough analysis sever the source of the reified ground!

།ཡོད་མ་མྱོང་བའི་རང་སྣང་ཡུལ་དུ་འཁྲུལ།

YOE	**MA**	**NYONG WAI**	**RANG NANG**	**YUL**	**DU**	**TRUL**
truly existing, real	*not*	*experienced*	*self-appearance, self luminosity,*	*object*	*as*	*confused*

Mind's intrinsic appearance has never existed yet it is erroneously taken to be an object.

།མ་རིག་དབང་གིས་རང་རིག་བདག་ཏུ་འཁྲུལ།

MA RIG	**WANG**	**GI**	**RANG RIG**	**DAG**	**TU**	**TRUL**
unawareness	*power*	*due to*	*reflexive awareness*	*self*	*as*	*confuse, bewilder*

Due to the power of unawareness, reflexive awareness is mistaken for oneself.

།གཉིས་འཛིན་དབང་གིས་སྲིད་པའི་ཀློང་དུ་འཁྱམས།

NYI	**DZIN**	**WANG**	**GI**	**SI PAI**	**LONG DU**	**CHAM**
dual	*holding,* believing*	*power*	*by*	*samsara, the realms of endless becoming*	*vastness*	*wander*

* subject and object as both real and separate

Due to the power of dualistic clinging we wander in the vastness of creation.

།མ་རིག་འཁྲུལ་པའི་རྩད་བདར་ཆོད་པར་ཤོག།

MA RIG	**TRUL PAI**	**TSAE**	**DAR**	**CHOE PAR**	**SHO**
unawareness, ignoring	*confusing*	*root*	*accurately, finely, completely*	*cut*	*may*

May we fully cut off unawareness, the source of delusion.

Intrinsic appearance has no existence yet is mistaken for an object.
Intrinsic awareness, due to the power of unawareness,
Is mistaken for oneself.
The power of clinging to duality
Sets us wandering in the vastness of becoming.
May we cut off unawareness, the source of delusion!

།ཡོད་པ་མ་ཡིན་རྒྱལ་བས་ཀྱང་མ་གཟིགས།

YOE PA	**MA YIN**	**GYAL WAE**	**KYANG**	**MA**	**ZI**
exists, real	*is not*	*jina, buddha*	*even*	*not*	*seen*

It is not existent, for even the buddhas cannot see it.

།མེད་པ་མ་ཡིན་འཁོར་འདས་ཀུན་གྱི་གཞི།

ME PA	**MA YIN**	**KHOR**	**DAE**	**KUN**	**GYI**	**ZHI**
nothing at all, not existing	*is not*	*samsara*	*nirvana*	*all*	*of*	*ground*

It is not non-existent, for it is the basis of all of samsara and nirvana.

།འགལ་འདུ་མ་ཡིན་ཟུང་འཇུག་དབུ་མའི་ལམ།

GAL	**DU**	**MA YIN**	**ZUNG JU**	**U MAI**	**LAM**
contradiction, dichotomy (not either, neither or both)	*association*	*is not (i.e. paradox)*	*conjoined, inseparable*	*middle, madhyamaka*	*path, way*

This is no paradox, being the non-dual union, the middle way.

།མཐའ་བྲལ་སེམས་ཀྱི་ཆོས་ཉིད་རྟོགས་པར་ཤོག།

THA	**DRAL**	**SEM**	**KYI**	**CHO NYI**	**TOG PAR**	**SHO**
*extreme**	*free of*	*mind*	*of*	*actuality*	*see clearly, awaken to*	*may*

*of existence and non-existence and so on

May we awaken to the actuality of mind free of extremes.

It is not existent, for even the buddhas cannot see it.
It is not non-existent, being the basis of samsara and nirvana.
This is no paradox, being the non-dual union, the middle way.
May we awaken to the actuality of this mind free of extremes!

།འདི་ཡིན་ཞེས་པ་གང་གིས་མཚོན་པ་མེད།

DI	**YIN**	**ZHE PA**	**GANG**	**GI**	**TSHON PA**	**ME**
this (being)	*is*	*said to be*	*whatever*	*by*	*sign, symbol, indication*	*without*

Nothing is indicated by saying, "it is this".

།འདི་མིན་ཞེས་བྱ་གང་གིས་བཀག་པ་མེད།

DI	**MIN**	**ZHE JA**	**GANG**	**GI**	**KAG PA**	**ME**
this (non being)	*is not*	*called*	*whatever*	*by*	*refute*	*without*

The referent of "it is not this" offers nothing to refute.

།བློ་ལས་འདས་པའི་ཆོས་ཉིད་འདུས་མ་བྱས།

LO	**LAE DAE PAI**	**CHO NYI**	**DUE MA JAE**
intellect	*beyond*	*actuality*	*uncompounded, not composite unconditioned, unfabricated*

Unfabricated actuality beyond the reach of intellect.

།ཡང་དག་དོན་གྱི་མཐའ་ནི་ངེས་པ་ཤོག།

YANG DA	**DON**	**GYI**	**THA NI**	**NGE PA**	**SHO**
completely pure	*meaning, ultimate*	*of*	*limit, final, ultimate*	*certain*	*may*

May we be certain in this unsurpassable final limit.

"This is it" finds nothing to indicate.
"This is not it" finds nothing to refute.
Unfabricated actuality beyond the reach of intellect.
May we be certain in this unsurpassable final limit.

།འདི་ཉིད་མ་རྟོགས་འཁོར་བའི་རྒྱ་མཚོར་འཁོར།

DI NYI	**MA**	**TO**	**KHOR WAI**	**GYAM**	**TSHO**	**KHOR**
this, actuality	*not*	*see, awaken to*	*samsara*	*ocean*		*revolve in*

Being unaware of this, we circle in the ocean of samsara.

།འདི་ཉིད་རྟོགས་ན་སངས་རྒྱས་གཞན་ན་མེད།

DI NYI	**TO**	**NA**	**SANG GYE**	**ZHEN**	**NA**	**ME**
this, actuality	*see, awaken to*	*if*	*buddha, enlightenment*	*other*	*than*	*not*

Awakening to this, there is no other enlightenment.

།ཐམས་ཅད་འདི་ཡིན་འདི་མིན་གང་ཡང་མེད།

THAM CHE	**DI**	**YIN**	**DI**	**MIN**	**GANG YANG**	**ME**
all	*this*	*is*	*this*	*is not*	*of anything whatsoever*	*without*

This is the whole of all there is, with nothing which is not this.

།ཆོས་ཉིད་ཀུན་གཞིའི་མཚང་ནི་རིག་པར་ཤོག།

CHO NYI	**KUN ZHI**	**TSHANG**	**NI**	**RIG PAR**	**SHO**
actuality, dharmata	*ground of all, emptiness*	*hidden*	*these*	*be aware of*	*may*

May we be aware of the hidden actuality, the ground of all.

Being unaware of this, we circle in samsara's ocean.
Awakening to this, there is no other enlightenment.
This is the whole, with nothing which is not this.
May we be aware of the hidden actuality, the ground of all!

།སྣང་ཡང་སེམས་ལ་སྟོང་ཡང་སེམས་ཡིན་ཏེ།

NANG	YANG	SEM	LA	TONG	YANG	SEM	YIN	TE
appearing showing	*yet, if, whether*	*mind*	*to*	*empty*	*yet, if, whether*	*mind*	*is*	*hence, thus*

With appearance, there's the mind; with emptiness, there's the mind.

།རྟོགས་ཀྱང་སེམས་ལ་འཁྲུལ་ཡང་རང་གི་སེམས།

TO	KYANG	SEM	LA	TRUL	YANG	RANG GI	SEM
see, awaken to	*yet, whether*	*mind*	*to, as*	*confusion, delusion*	*yet, whether*	*own*	*mind*

With awakening, there's the mind; with confusion, there's also my mind.

།སྐྱེས་ཀྱང་སེམས་ལ་འགགས་ཀྱང་སེམས་ཡིན་པས།

KYE	KYANG	SEM	LA	GA	KYANG	SEM	YIN	PAE
arising, birth	*also, even*	*mind*	*as*	*ceasing*	*also*	*mind*	*is*	*therefore*

With arising, there's the mind; with ceasing, there's the mind.

།སྒྲོ་འདོགས་ཐམས་ཅད་སེམས་ལ་ཆོད་པར་ཤོག།

DRO DO	THAM CHE	SEM	LA	CHO PAR	SHO
doubts, interpretations	*all*	*mind*	*on, in*	*cut*	*may*

May we sever all interpretations within the mind.

Appearance is mind and emptiness also is mind.
Awakening is mind and delusion also is my mind.
Arising is mind and ceasing is mind.
May we sever all differentiating assertions within our mind!

།བློ་བྱས་རྩོལ་བའི་སྒོམ་གྱིས་མ་བསླད་ཅིང་།

LO	JAE	TSOL WAI	GOM	GYI	MA	LAE JING
intellect fabricate	*doing*	*effortful, deliberate*	*meditation*	*by*	*not*	*mixing, adulterating*

Not adulterated by effortful meditation employing the intellect, and

།ཐ་མལ་འདུ་འཛིའི་རླུང་གིས་མི་བསྐྱོད་པར།

THA MAL	DU DZI	LUNG	GI	MI KYOE PA
ordinary, common	*bustle, commotion*	*winds, volatility*	*by*	*undisturbed*

Unmoved by the volatility of the bustle of ordinary concerns,

།མ་བཅོས་གཉུག་མར་རང་བབ་འཇོག་ཤེས་པའི།

MA CHOE	NYUG MAR	RANG BAB	JOG	SHE PAI
uncontrived	*primordial, given*	*as it comes, flowing naturally*	*rest in,*	*knowing be in*

Knowing how to rest in uncontrived original free flow,

།སེམས་དོན་ཉམས་ལེན་མཁས་ཤིང་སྐྱོང་བར་ཤོག།

SEM	DON	NYAM LEN	KHAE SHING	KYONG WAR	SHO
mind	*meaning, key point*	*practice*	*knowledgeable, experienced*	*protect, sustain*	*may*

May we expertly protect our practice of the mind as it is.

Not corrupted by effortful mind-made meditation,
Undisturbed by the gusts of worldly concerns,
Knowing how to rest in uncontrived original free flow,
May we expertly maintain our practice of our mind as it is!

།ཕྲ་རགས་རྟོག་པའི་རྦ་རླབས་རང་སར་ཞི།

TRA	RA	TO PAI	BA LAB	RANG SAR	ZHI
subtle, fine	*rough, coarse*	*thoughts, concepts*	*waves*	*own place, by themselves*	*pacify, settle, still*

The waves of subtle and coarse thoughts subside where they are.

།གཡོ་མེད་སེམས་ཀྱི་ཆུ་བོ་ངང་གིས་གནས།

YOE	ME	SEM	KYI	CHU WO	NGANG	GI	NAE
movement undercurrent	*without*	*mind*	*of*	*stream,*	*own nature*	*by*	*settle, abide*

The water of undisturbed mind settles according to its own nature.

།བྱིང་རྨུགས་རྙོག་པའི་དྲི་མ་དང་བྲལ་བའི།

JING	MU	NYO PAI	DRI MA	DANG	DRAL WAI
sinking, torpor	*dull*	*silt, scum, turbidity*	*stain, pollution*	*and*	*free of*

Free of the staining turbidity of sinking and dullness

།ཞི་གནས་རྒྱ་མཚོ་མི་གཡོ་བརྟན་པར་ཤོག།

ZHI NAE	GYAM TSHO	MI YO	TAN PAR	SHO
calm, shamatha	*ocean*	*unwavering, unperturbed*	*stable, steady*	*may*

May the ocean of tranquillity be steady and undisturbed.

The waves of subtle and coarse thoughts subside by themselves.
The waters of undisturbed mind come naturally to rest.
Free of the staining turbidity of sinking and dullness
May the ocean of calm abiding be steady and unperturbed!

།བལྟར་མེད་སེམས་ལ་ཡང་ཡང་བལྟས་པའི་ཚེ།

TAR	**ME**	**SEM**	**LA**	**YANG YANG**	**TAE PAI**	**TSHE**
be seen	*without*	*mind*	*to*	*again and again*	*look*	*when*

When looking again and again at the invisible mind,

།མཐོང་མེད་དོན་ནི་ཇི་བཞིན་ལྷག་གེར་མཐོང་།

THONG	**ME**	**DON NI**	**JI ZHIN**	**LHA GER**	**THONG**
seeing	*without*	*meaning, fact, truth*	*as it is, truth of it*	*distinctly, vividly*	*see*

The unseeable ultimate is seen distinctly, just as it is.

།ཡིན་མིན་དོན་ལ་ཐེ་ཚོམ་ཆོད་པ་ཉིད།

YIN	**MIN**	**DON**	**LA**	**THE TSHOM**	**CHOE PA NYI**
is	*is not*	*truth as is*	*towards*	*doubts*	*cut fully*

This severs all the uncertainties of is and is not concerning the true, as is.

།འཁྲུལ་མེད་རང་ངོ་རང་གིས་ཤེས་པར་ཤོག།

TRUL ME	**RANG NGO**	**RANG GI**	**SHE PAR**	**SHO**
without confusion, undeluded	*own face, own essence*	*reflexively, by self, instant*	*know*	*may*

May we ourselves know our own essence free of delusion.

When looking repeatedly at the invisible mind,
The unseeable ultimate is seen distinctly, just as it is.
Severing uncertainty whether the true is or is not,
May we ourselves know our own essence free of delusion!

།ཡུལ་ལ་བལྟས་པས་ཡུལ་མེད་སེམས་སུ་མཐོང་།

YUL	**LA**	**TAE PAE**	**YUL**	**ME**	**SEM**	**SU**	**THONG**
object	*at*	*by looking*	*object*	*without*	*mind*	*as, at with*	*see*

Looking at an object, we see no object, just mind.

།སེམས་ལ་བལྟས་པས་སེམས་མེད་ངོ་བོ་སྟོང་།

SEM	**LA**	**TAE PAE**	**SEM**	**ME**	**NGO WO**	**TONG**
mind	*for*	*by looking*	*mind*	*without*	*essence*	*empty*

Looking for mind, we see no mind, only the empty essence.

།གཉིས་ལ་བལྟས་པས་གཉིས་འཛིན་རང་སར་གྲོལ།

NYI	**LA**	**TAE PAE**	**NYI DZIN**	**RANG SAR**	**DROL**
two, both	*at*	*by looking*	*dualism*	*own place, where it is*	*liberated, vanishes*

Looking at both, clinging to duality is liberated where it is.

།འོད་གསལ་སེམས་ཀྱི་གནས་ལུགས་རྟོགས་པར་ཤོག།

OE SAL	**SEM**	**KYI**	**NAE LU**	**TO PAR**	**SHO**
lustrous, luminosity	*mind*	*of*	*as it is, givenness*	*see, awaken to*	*may*

May we awaken to luminosity, the givenness of mind.

Looking at an object, there is no object: I see it is my mind.
Looking for mind, there is no mind, for it is empty essence.
Looking at both, clinging to duality is self-liberated.
May we awaken to luminosity, the givenness of mind!

།ཡིད་བྱེད་བྲལ་བ་འདི་ནི་ཕྱག་རྒྱ་ཆེ།

YI JE	**DRAL WA**	**DI NI**	**CHA GYA**	**CHE**
mental activity, construction	*free of*	*this*	*mahamudra, given, what is*	*great*

Separate from mental activity, this is the great mahamudra.

།མཐའ་དང་བྲལ་བ་དབུ་མ་ཆེན་པོ་ཡིན།

THA	**DANG**	**DRAL WA**	**U MA**	**CHEN PO**	**YIN**
limits	*free of*		*madhyamaka*	*great*	*is*

Free of extremes, this is the great middle way.

།འདི་ནི་ཀུན་འདུས་རྫོགས་ཆེན་ཞེས་ཀྱང་བྱ།

DI NI	**KUN**	**DUE**	**DZO CHEN**	**ZHE**	**KYANG**	**JA**
this	*all*	*include, encompassing*	*dzogchen, great completion*	*called*	*also*	*is*

Inclusive of all, it is also known as the great completion.

།གཅིག་ཤེས་ཀུན་དོན་རྟོགས་པའི་གདེངས་ཐོབ་ཤོག །

CHI	**SHE**	**KUN**	**DON**	**TO PAI**	**DENG**	**TO**	**SHO**
one	*know*	*all*	*meaning*	*see, awaken*	*confidence*	*gain*	*may to*

May we gain the confidence of awakening to knowing one as the meaning of all.

Unmade by mental activity, this is the great mahamudra.
Free from extremes, this is the great middle way.
Inclusive of all, it is also called the great completion.
May we be confident in awakening to knowing one as the truth of all!

།ཞེན་པ་མེད་པའི་བདེ་ཆེན་རྒྱུན་ཆད་མེད།

ZHEN PA	**ME PAI**	**DE CHEN**	**GYUN CHA ME**
desire, clinging	*without*	*great bliss, happiness*	*unceasing, uninterrupted flow, continuous*

Great bliss free of attachment is unceasing.

།མཚན་འཛིན་མེད་པའི་འོད་གསལ་སྒྲིབ་གཡོགས་བྲལ།

TSHEN	**DZIN**	**ME PAI**	**OE SAL**	**DRIB**	**YO**	**DRAL**
defining characteristics	*grasping, relying on*	*without*	*clarity, clear light*	*obscuration*	*veil*	*free of*

Luminosity free of grasping at characteristics is unobscured.

།བློ་ལས་འདས་པའི་མི་རྟོག་ལྷུན་གྱིས་གྲུབ།

LO LAE	**DAE PA**	**MI TO**	**LHUN GYI DRU**
intellect	*gone beyond*	*non-conceptuality, no thought*	*effortlessly arising, instant presence*

Non-conceptuality beyond intellect is instant presence.

།རྩོལ་མེད་ཉམས་མྱོང་རྒྱུན་ཆད་མེད་པར་ཤོག།

TSOL ME	**NYAM**	**NYONG**	**GYUN CHA ME PAR**	**SHO**
without effort, unsought	*meditation states**	*experience*	*uninterrupted, continuity*	*may*

*bliss, luminosity, no thought

May unelicited meditative experiences occur without interruption.

Great bliss free of attachment is continuous.
Luminosity free of reliance on characteristics is unobscured.
Non-thought, beyond concept, is instantly present.
May these unelicited experiences be continuous!

།བཟང་ཞེན་ཉམས་ཀྱི་འཛིན་པ་རང་སར་གྲོལ།

ZANG	**ZHEN**	**NYAM**	**KYI**	**DZIN PA**	**RANG SAR**	**DROL**
*good states**	*clinging*	*meditation*	*of*	*grasping*	*own place, where they are, on the spot*	*liberate, go free*

* in particular, bliss, clarity and no-thought

Grasping at 'good' meditation experiences is liberated in its own place.

།ངན་རྟོག་འཁྲུལ་པ་རང་བཞིན་དབྱིངས་སུ་དག།

NGAN	**TO**	**TRUL PA**	**RANG ZHIN**	**YING**	**SU**	**DA**
bad	*thought*	*delusion*	*its nature*	*dharmadhatu*	*in*	*pure*

Delusional 'bad thoughts' are inherently pure within all-encompassing space.

།ཐ་མལ་ཤེས་པ་སྤང་བླང་བྲལ་ཐོབ་མེད།

THA MAL	**SHE PA**	**PANG**	**LANG**	**DRAL**	**TO**	**ME**
ordinary, unaltered	*knowing, consciousness*	*discard*	*adopt*	*parting from*	*gaining, add*	*without*

Ordinary mind is beyond discarding and adopting, removing and adding.

།སྤྲོས་བྲལ་ཆོས་ཉིད་བདེན་པ་རྟོགས་པར་ཤོག།

TOE DRAL	**CHO NYI**	**DEN PA**	**TO PAR**	**SHO**
free of interpretation or elaboration	*actuality*	*truth*	*awaken to*	*may*

May we awaken to the truth of actuality beyond interpretation.

Attachment to 'good' meditation is self-liberated.
Delusional 'bad' thoughts are inherently pure in the space of phenomena.
Intrinsic mind is beyond adopting or discarding, adding or subtracting.
May we awaken to the truth of the actual, free of limiting constructs!

།འགྲོ་བའི་རང་བཞིན་རྟག་ཏུ་སངས་རྒྱས་ཀྱང་།

DRO WAI	**RANG ZHIN**	**TAG TU**	**SANG GYE**	**KYANG**
sentient beings wanderers	*nature*	*always*	*buddha, awakened*	*yet*

Although the true nature of all sentient beings is always enlightened,

།མ་རྟོགས་དབང་གིས་མཐའ་མེད་འཁོར་བར་འཁྱམས།

MA TO	**WANG**	**GI**	**THA ME**	**KHOR WAR**	**CHAM**
not seeing	*power*	*by*	*without limit*	*samsara*	*wander*

Due to the power of not awakening to this they wander in endless samsara.

།སྡུག་བསྔལ་མུ་མཐའ་མེད་པའི་སེམས་ཅན་ལ།

DU NGAL	**MU THA**	**ME PAI**	**SEM CHEN**	**LA**
suffering, misery	*boundary, limit*	*without*	*sentient beings*	*to*

Towards these sentient beings whose suffering is without limit

།བཟོད་མེད་སྙིང་རྗེ་རྒྱུད་ལ་སྐྱེ་བར་ཤོག།

ZO ME	**NYING JE**	**GYU**	**LA**	**KYE WAR**	**SHO**
intense, overwhelming	*compassion*	*mind stream*	*in*	*be born, arise*	*may*

May unbearable compassion arise in our mind.

The true nature of all beings is always enlightened,
Yet, unaware of this, they wander endlessly in samsara.
Towards these beings whose suffering is without limit
May intense compassion arise within us!

།བཟོད་མེད་སྙིང་རྗེའི་རྩལ་ཡང་མ་འགགས་པའི།

ZOE ME	**NYING JEI**	**TSAL**	**YANG**	**MA GA PAI**
uncontainable	*compassion*	*energy*	*also*	*without cease, uninterrupted*

When the energy of uncontainable compassion flows as ceaseless love

།བརྩེ་དུས་ངོ་བོ་སྟོང་དོན་རྗེན་པར་ཤར།

TSE	**DUE**	**NGO WO**	**TONG**	**DON**	**JEN PAR**	**SHAR**
affection, kindness	*while, when*	*essence*	*empty*	*meaning, wisdom*	*nakedly, clearly*	*arise*

The fact of its empty essence is nakedly apparent.

།ཟུང་འཇུག་གོལ་ས་བྲལ་བའི་ལམ་མཆོག་འདི།

ZUNG JU	**GOL**	**SA**	**DRAL WAI**	**LAM**	**CHO**	**DI**
*conjunction inseparable union**	*error, deviation*	*site*	*free of*	*path*	*supreme*	*this*

* of wisdom and compassion

From this union, the supreme path free of error,

།འབྲལ་མེད་ཉིན་མཚན་ཀུན་ཏུ་བསྒོམ་པར་ཤོག།

DRAL ME	**NYIN**	**TSHEN**	**KUN TU**	**GOM PAR**	**SHO**
never separate present in	*day*	*night*	*always*	*meditate, be*	*may*

May we never separate, and practise always by day and by night.

When the energy of uncontainable compassion flows as endless love
The fact of its empty essence is nakedly apparent.
This union is the supreme path free of error.
May this be our ceaseless presence by day and by night!

།སྒོམ་སྟོབས་ལས་བྱུང་སྤྱན་དང་མངོན་ཤེས་དང་།

GOM	TO	LAE	JUNG	CHEN	DANG	NGON SHE	DANG
meditation	*strength, power*	*from*	*arising*	*eye**	*and*	*clear knowing, extra ordinary knowing*	*and*

* the five wisdom eyes of a buddha

From the power of meditation we gain wisdom eyes and clairvoyant perception, and

།སེམས་ཅན་སྨིན་བྱས་སངས་རྒྱས་ཞིང་རབ་སྦྱངས།

SEM CHEN	MIN JAE	SANG GYE	ZHING	RAB	JANG
sentient beings awakened	*ripened*	*buddha, field*	*realm,*	*fully*	*purified, refined*

We ripen sentient beings, purify buddha-fields, and

།སངས་རྒྱས་ཆོས་རྣམས་འགྲུབ་པའི་སྨོན་ལམ་རྫོགས།

SANG GYE	CHO NAM	DRU PAI	MON LAM	DZO
buddha	*dharmas, qualities*	*actualise, accomplish*	*aspiration*	*fulfilled*

Fulfil our aspiration to attain the qualities of a buddha.

།རྫོགས་སྨིན་སྦྱངས་གསུམ་མཐར་ཕྱིན་སངས་རྒྱས་ཤོག།

DZO	MIN	JANG	SUM	THAR CHIN	SANG GYE	SHO
perfect, completing	*ripening*	*purifying, cleansing*	*three*	*fulfil, complete*	*buddha*	*may*

By completing this fulfilling, ripening and purifying may we attain buddhahood.

By the power of meditation, wisdom eyes and clairvoyance arise, and we
Ripen sentient beings, purify our buddha-fields and
Fulfil our aspirations to attain the qualities of a buddha.
By completing this fulfilment, maturation and cleansing
May we attain buddhahood!

།ཕྱོགས་བཅུའི་རྒྱལ་བ་སྲས་བཅས་ཐུགས་རྗེ་དང་།

CHO	**CHU**	**GYAL WA**	**SAE CHAE**	**THU JE**	**DANG**
directions (everywhere)	*ten*	*jinas, buddhas*	*bodhisattvas, spiritual offspring*	*compassion, kindness*	*and*

By the power of the compassion of the victors and bodhisattvas of the ten directions, and

།རྣམ་དཀར་དགེ་བ་ཇི་སྙེད་ཡོད་པའི་མཐུས།

NAM KAR	**GE WA**	**JI NYE**	**YOE PAI**	**THUE**
pure	*virtue*	*as much as there is*	*possess*	*by power or force of*

By the power of all pure virtue, as much as there is,

།དེ་ལྟར་བདག་དང་སེམས་ཅན་ཐམས་ཅད་ཀྱི།

DE TAR	**DA**	**DANG**	**SEM CHEN**	**THAM CHE**	**KYI**
like that	*I*	*and*	*sentient beings*	*all*	*of*

May this pure aspiration of myself and all sentient beings

།སྨོན་ལམ་རྣམ་དག་ཇི་བཞིན་འགྲུབ་གྱུར་ཅིག།

MON LAM	**NAM DA**	**JI ZHIN**	**DRUB GYUR**	**CHI**
aspiration, good wishes	*pure*	*as it is made*	*accomplished*	*be*

Be accomplished exactly as we intend.

By the power of the compassion
Of all buddhas and bodhisattvas everywhere, and
The power of all pure virtue, as much as there is,
May this pure aspiration I share with all beings
Be accomplished just as we intend!

Every day I'm catching
                    what can't be caught
Everyday my effort
                    comes to naught
Illusion piled on illusion
                    forms not a single drop
Yet since I'm catching nothing
                    why should I stop